Food , Energy , and Water

I0475575

Fᴏᴏᴅ   Eɴᴇʀɢʏ   Wᴀᴛᴇʀ

Tʜᴇ   Fᴏᴜɴᴅᴀᴛɪᴏɴ   Sʏsᴛᴇᴍs   ᴏꜰ
Mᴏᴅᴇʀɴ Sᴏᴄɪᴇᴛʏ

ARTHUR JACKSON

Food Energy Water: The Foundation Systems of Modern Society
Copyright © 2007 Arthur Jackson

ISBN: 978-1-300-27659-3
Arthur Jackson
4708 87th Street S.W.
Mukilteo, WA

ALL RIGHTS RESERVED. This book may not be reproduced in whole, or in part, by any means, without the written consent of the publisher.

Any trademarks referred to within this publication are the property of their respective trademark holders. None of these trademark holders are affiliated with the Publisher, their products, or website.

PRINTED IN THE UNITED STATES OF AMERICA.

Food , Energy , and Water

ARTHUR JACKSON

Other works by Arthur Jackson
Non-fiction:

Chaos, Synchronicity, and Capitalism:
The Phases in the Evolution of a Natural System (2006)

The Ethics of Ethics (2005)

Fiction :

Westfall (2004)
Purity (2005)
Knights of the First Order (2006)
Shadows   (2008)

Food , Energy , and Water

Table of Contents

ARTHUR JACKSON

Tables

Food , Energy , and Water

7

ARTHUR JACKSON

Table of Figures

Preface

It is often those innocent questions sparked by the wonder of youth that shape our curiosity and the forces that will drive that curiosity in us as adults. Why does our society or any society function as it does? Many of the activities were established by social systems created in the past and are currently being maintained by the larger society. Other organized patterns of behavior seemed to have occurred spontaneously, without any specific organizing effort, but continue to control and govern behavior for very long periods of time. Take the case of the local farmer. Why does he favor certain crops and not others? Why are certain animals used for domestic stock and not others? Why is the method of farming in China and India so different from farming in America and Europe? Why are there so many more people in Asia and India than in the rest of the world? Was there some guiding principle that determined which patterns of behavior would dominate? To understand these process one must first understand the layers of systems controlling our world.

ARTHUR JACKSON

Modern society rests upon a primary layer of systems composed of three distinct foundation systems, or pillars that came into existence over many hundreds of thousands to perhaps millions of years; Food, Energy, and Water. The stability of each of these pillars is critical to the survival of human societies. Throughout this book, I will look at each of these pillars, or foundation systems from their origins to their status in today's world. This historical overview will provide insight into how societies evolved within these systems, but more importantly how they remain stable, a critical requirement for long-term survival. The evolution of these systems is often viewed differently depending upon your perspective.   The biological sciences look to genetic material, and physical development, as just some of the criteria in evaluating such systems. Economists are more concerned with an approach used to evaluate how these forces interact for survival and longevity. As an engineer, I will try to walk a middle ground between these disciplines, and view them as a systems engineer.

Many of these systems have evolved around humanity and continue to evolve with human society, becoming more complex, as the demands upon the systems increase. This rise in demand has placed increasing amounts of stress on each of these foundation pillars that may have long ranging impacts for human society. In this first book I look at first order, or primary systems, those very long lived systems, which have evolved through natural forces around mankind, and are necessary for human survival. In subsequent books I will extend this analysis to second order systems, which have life spans measured in hundreds to thousands of years, which are created by humans and have significant impact on primary systems. Finally in book three we will look to third order systems that frenetic froth composed of systems with life spans of years or less that shape modern behavior. But now let us begin this process with the study of the critical primary systems.

ARTHUR JACKSON

FOOD

The original system

The Ice Age

The advance and decline of ice sheets over the face of the planet has played an important part in the evolution of human society; until recently, exactly how important was unclear. We now have begun to understand that the pattern of movement of glaciers in ice ages has been pivotal in setting the stage for a specific type of development in human societies. Starting about 34 million years ago, during a period of planetary cooling, polar-regions of our planet began to form. The formation of a permanent ice covered region is very important, as is exactly how much of the planet was covered by this region. This has been a contention of much debate. At one point, there was a theory put forward called, "Snowball Earth," (Hoffman, 1999)which made an argument that at some point the entire surface of the planet earth was covered by ice sheets. Geologist using analysis of glacial sedimentary rock formations in parts of the Middle East have been able to trace the cycles of hot and cold to about 850 to 540 million year ago. Using a complex technique known as, Chemical Index of Alteration, the teams were able to examine sedimentary rocks for evidence of climate change. These researchers found evidence of intervals of extremely low temperature, or very cold climate, which alternated with high temperature activity. These cycles of activity provide a clear indication that a complete deep freeze as suggested by the, "Snowball earth" theory never took place. Despite severe glaciations at different times throughout its history, there was never a period of time when the entire surface would be covered with ice. There were always areas of unfrozen ocean as well as areas of the land mass that would not have been covered by glacial activity. This research has added a great deal of information to the ongoing debate about climate change, not only in the past, but in the present-day.

"If the earth had become fully frozen for a long period of time, these climatic cycles could not exist and the Earth would have changed into a bleak world with almost no weather, since no water evaporation from the oceans could take place, and little snowfall would be possible. In fact, once fully frozen it is difficult to create the right conditions to cause weather patterns, since most of the incoming solar radiation would be reflected back by the snow and ice. The evidence of climate cycles is therefore hostile to the idea of "Snowball earth"". (Imperial College of London, (2007))

Food , Energy , and Water

The examination of this theory raises import questions about how ice fields proceeded, and receded over the distant past.

The Antarctic icecap grew into existence approximately 35 million years ago, and became established only about 2.4 million years ago (Hewitt G. , 2000). From the creation of the Arctic icecap until 0.9 million years ago, ice sheets advanced and receded in cycles of approximately 41,000 years. These cycles continued, with some gradual change, to become a 100,000 year cycle. The reason for this increase in the cycle time frame is based upon the Croll-Milankovitch theory of orbital eccentricity in Earth's orbit around the sun. This theory identifies a main orbital eccentricity, of every 100,000 years, a variation in the earth's axial tilt that occurs approximately every 41,000 years and the precession to the earth's axis wobble, which has a period of roughly 19 to 23,000 years. The effect of these variations upon the energy transfer between the earth and sun led to significant climate changes. Hewitt analyzed ice cores of two (2) kiloliters in establishing these variations. This also identifies periods of oscillation and variations with in the 100,000 years cycle. Sheets of ice would advance from the Polar Regions and cover significant portions of the earth's surface, with a consequent dramatic impact on resources available to plants and animals existing at the time. (Williams, 1998)

We now understand that an ice age comes into existence when ice fields advance from the Polar Regions to cover approximately 40 percent of the planet's surface area. During these periods of oscillation, the polar ice sheets expand considerably with these changes in temperatures. This results in a compression of marine life forms, animal life and vegetation toward the equator. It also would create a change in water content available for plants and animals to use for survival. When ice sheets advance much of the available water is then locked up in the sheets themselves. This would create some arid zones where survival of plant and animal species would be difficult. The most favorable areas of plant and animal survival are largely considered the leading edge of the ice fields. There would be concentrations of animal species and plant species in these areas where there would be available sources of water. Species of plants and animals would be quick to adapt to this habitable region and establish themselves, only to find their existence placed in question as the oscillatory movement of ice sheets changed their environment, as they would recede. (Hewitt G. M., 1996) The first time this occurred there would be a dramatic increase of species to accommodate the increase in the usable land mass available for both plants and animals, as more water was liberated. This would have occurred at a rapid rate for some species. However, as the next cycle of ice field expansion would began, species would find themselves once again compressed toward the equator with much of their land mass covered with ice, and much of the remainder now being too arid to sustain either plants or animals. This would have resulted in very different survival patterns between plants and animals.

For plants, this would have produced some hard ship, but would not have necessarily been detrimental to the existence of an individual species. Many species of plants would be able to lay dormant, waiting for the gradual retreat of the ice sheets to allow them to restart their existence. (Gray, 1997) The movement of ice sheets will have provided the transport mechanism for many plant species. As glaciers moved to the father limit of their expansion, and began the inevitable process of recession, the seeds would be deposited into areas that would soon become able to sustain plant life. (Colinvaux, 1996)This process would be repeated many times. This leading edge expansion, in theory, would make it possible for plant species of many different varieties to become located in the same areas. Modeling and simulation of such expansions have helped to validate this process. It is important to note that this leading-edge expansion created competition among species. The first populations to occupy and disperse over fertile regions would act as a deterrent to other species, forcing them to reproduce logistically and not exponentially like the original. The result would be the creation of boundaries between different species that would continue to exist for some time. It also makes it clear that as the ice fields would advance the species would suffer shrinkage, dedication, and extinction, becoming bottlenecked. With the next cycle, plants that had survived would find themselves in a different environment. The conditions of soil, light, and climate would not be a mirror image of what existed. This would tend to create more favorable conditions for some species as opposed to others, allowing them to spread more rapidly into favorable conditions. The result would have been an increase in diversity each time the ice field advanced, and subsequently retreated. This is supported by experimental work in the study of flies, which shows an increase in genetic variants with severe bottlenecks. This process would be repeated by plant species across large parts of Europe and North America. (Wade, 1998) However, the survival rate of species would be dependent upon geographical location, and specific climate conditions. In Europe, its geographical placement of large land masses along preferable meridians' would act as an incentive for the collection of a number of these plants species over time.

For animals the process would have been more severe. The movement of ice sheets which have been a significant problem for many species of animal including humans. Studies in recent years have indicated the existence of genetic bottlenecks with in human populations caused by these relocations. (Ambrose, 1998) When first discovered this process was largely considered to be an anomaly, but has now been revealed to be a recurring pattern of activity within the species. As usable surface area would be decreased with the advance of ice sheets, animal populations would be reduced to accommodate the smaller area and food sources. This would create a fierce competition between species for survival. Again, the favorable geographic placement of landmasses of Europe and the Middle East provide explanation as to why many species were able to survive in this region that disappeared in North America. (Diamond, 1999) These oscillations would make it necessary for species to be able to move and adapt, or go extinct.

With these repeated climate oscillations and changes, animal populations would pass through many stages of reorganization, and the genetic structure of groups would change radically. One of the most significant changes to have occurred within the animal kingdom would be the emergence of man. The historical record recognizes bones and tools of

Homo erectus being found in Africa and over Asia from a timeframe dating back 1.5 million years ago. Within this timeframe we see the emergence of Neanderthals in Europe from 300,000 years ago. DNA testing has established a divergence of this species from the main family of humans at around 600,000 years ago. Although this particular divergence in the human genome did not produce a viable group it does provide substantial support to the genetic diversity created by glacial movements. Neanderthals were ideally suited to the cold climate produced by glacial advance. The intelligence of Neanderthals has often been considered to be equivalent to that of modern man (Lewin, 1988). Despite these advantages it would not be Neanderthal that would become the dominant species.

At around 200,000 years ago we see the emergence of another diverse human species, modern man. Modern humans began the advance from simple creatures of the herd to intelligent beings. Groups of humans would emerge from Africa and gradually begin the formation of hunter gatherer groups. These groups would develop new technologies, and new social structures that would enable them to survive where other members of the diverse human population would not. The inevitable advance of glaciers would prove a hardship for this new and diverging group during times of glacial advance.

Populations of human hunter gatherer groups would be reduced in size to near extinction. Recent studies of molecular genetic diversity in contemporary populations suggest a reduction in population size to about 10,000 humans during the period of time termed a long genetic bottle neck or population bottleneck, which coincides well with periods of increased glacial activity. (Lahr, 1996). The genetic bottle neck is a significant reduction in population that can cause the extinction of a genetic lineage within the population. This often decreases genetic diversity. Population bottle necks are not new. They have occurred many times throughout the history of this planet in most animals and plants. As a result of these population bottle necks, human populations have less genetic diversity than their closest living relative, the chimpanzee.

The last population bottle neck can be traced back to a period of time roughly 40,000 years ago, and coincides with the appearance of advanced tool technologies and changes in the social structure of modern humans. These changes and adaptations occurred during the period termed the Middle Stone Age, and may have been instrumental in facilitating population expansion and colonization by increasing the chances of survival in arid regions during glacial advancements. These new technologies would increase efficiency and enlarged the available food supply. They would also foster cooperation between different hunter gatherer groups, and result in the exchange of technologies, as well as social and cultural exchanges as the groups would often meet to cooperate in hunting, gathering and forging. This would have enhanced and encouraged social and technological innovations that may have facilitated population expansion in side Africa, and dispersal out of Africa.

Sometime around 41,000 years ago modern man entered Europe and the Fertile Crescent with new technology and social structure that allowed them to spread across the region displacing Neanderthals.

Hunter Gatherers

Human history spans approximately 3 million years. During much of this time, human evolution parallels development in the animal kingdom. As the forces of climate have helped shaped the diversity of many species of animals on the planet, it has had a similar impact on human populations. We do not know at exactly what point humans moved from simple creatures of the herd to the more sophisticated groups of hunter-gatherer only that this process was a long and continuous path of evolutionary development.

The early part of this development would have been changes in body mass and body type engendered by a radical change in climate conditions. Changes in body type are fundamental to the new role of humans as hunter gathers, and in response to changing temperatures brought on by climate variations. Two very recent studies building on the concept of "Allen's rule" have increased our understanding of how temperature variations result in changes in body style and type in animal populations (Allen J. A., 1877). Allen's rule simply stated suggests that changes in body mass occur in response to external temperature. The colder the climate, the heavier and stockier the body type to accommodate internal temperature regulation and control. This greater body mass is a process of reducing heat loss. Consequently during periods of global warming, species tend to decrease body mass, and increase limbs size and structure as a way of accelerating the dissipation of heat during warmer temperatures. Studies by Bergman in predicting changes in body size, and in corresponding changes in body shape have supported these findings (Roberts, 1953). These were some of the changes that would impact humans and animals as they move through changing climate fluctuations. Animal populations were being physically and genetically altered in response to changes in climate. A study by Roberts correlated changes in overall stature and weight of human populations with mean change in temperature. Understanding that climate shift created alterations in the physical structure of the animal species brings us to the question of how did the shifts impact the social and psychological structure of species.

Throughout the entirety of the three million years of their existence, mankind has functioned more or less as all other animal species, carrying out the basic instincts of survival and the activities associated with survival. All animal species to a degree are hunters and gatherers. It is not unusual, nor should be viewed as unusual, when we talk about animal populations that engage in group activities. There are well documented studies evaluating group behavior among such social species as lions, wolves, and other predators, as well as group activities among non predatory species. This activity has also been well documented in insect populations such as bees that cooperate in the collection and processing of pollen. Collective activity among species is a natural process. It was this process at some point during human evolution that moved mankind on a separate and distinct path from other species of mammals. Humans began to diverge not only in terms of their physical characteristics, but also in terms of their psychological and social make up. By the time we reach 250,000 years ago, humans had successfully diverged from other mammals to become a distinct and separate group in terms of physical characteristics, and in terms of their psychology and sociology. They became a distinct group that interacted with other groups of animals and plants in a new social structure. Humans were developing into the first organized groups of hunters and gatherers with a psychology different from other groups of hunter gatherer species. The first significant difference was in human interaction with plants and other groups of animals. The process of hunting and gathering for humans became a sophisticated movement toward specialization utilizing modern technologies. Humans began to develop techniques that far surpassed other species in both efficiency and lethality. This process was aided by very subtle changes in their social structure. They gradually became the first species not limited by food sources, and apart from the rest of the animal and plant kingdoms as the following figure shows.

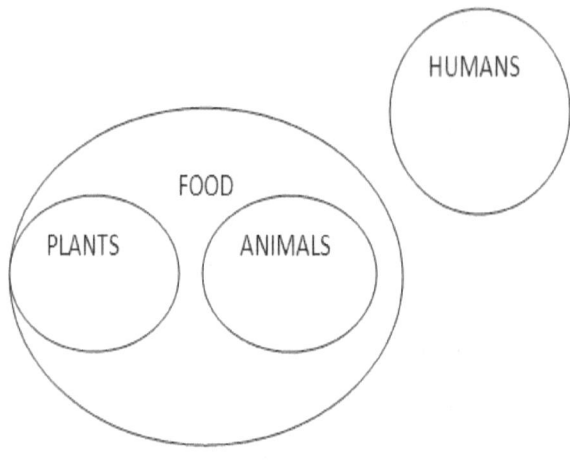

Figure 1 The relationships of independent groups in the hunter gatherer system

This new relationship would help to structure the future development of human hunter gatherer groups. The slow process of movement down this path of divergence also created unexpected benefits. Over the last several cycles of climate activity humans had experienced the same bottle neck in their gene pool. Radical changes in climate activity resulted in drastic reductions in the number of humans in response to reductions plant and animals available during the colder time frames. As we move into the period of the last 50,000 years we begin to see a radical change in human behavior in the way humans interacted with their environment. Humans moved into a period of time when they would establish a system of stable food production. This process did not occur instantaneously. It was not an invention, nor was it a conscious choice. It was the creation of a new system that came into existence as a result of repetitive activity over a very long period of time. As we discussed earlier there are a number of different groups of animal species that engage in hunting and gathering. Each approached the situation differently, and has developed specialized skills around their particular approach to the problem of hunting and gathering. Human beings would develop a new concept in hunting and gathering that would be singular in its approach to the problem. There are a number of groups throughout the globe that engage in hunting and gathering even today. Jared Diamond in his best-selling novel, "Guns, Germs, and Steel" provided an overview of many such societies throughout the world. It is worthwhile repeating at this point a direct excerpt from his work.

> "What actually happened was not a discovery of food production, nor an invention, as we might first assume. There was often not even a conscious choice between food production and hunting-gathering. "

Guns, Germs and Steel, By Jared Diamond, W.W. Norton and company, 1999, page 105

The move to food production rather than hunting and gathering was an important development and change in the social and psychological structure of human society. Humans were establishing a system that operated with selective exclusion. This human activity would lead to the creation of a system that would have a profound impact on human evolution. The steps leading to this development are identified in Figure 2. This is the generally accepted model for Europe.

Figure 2 The European Model

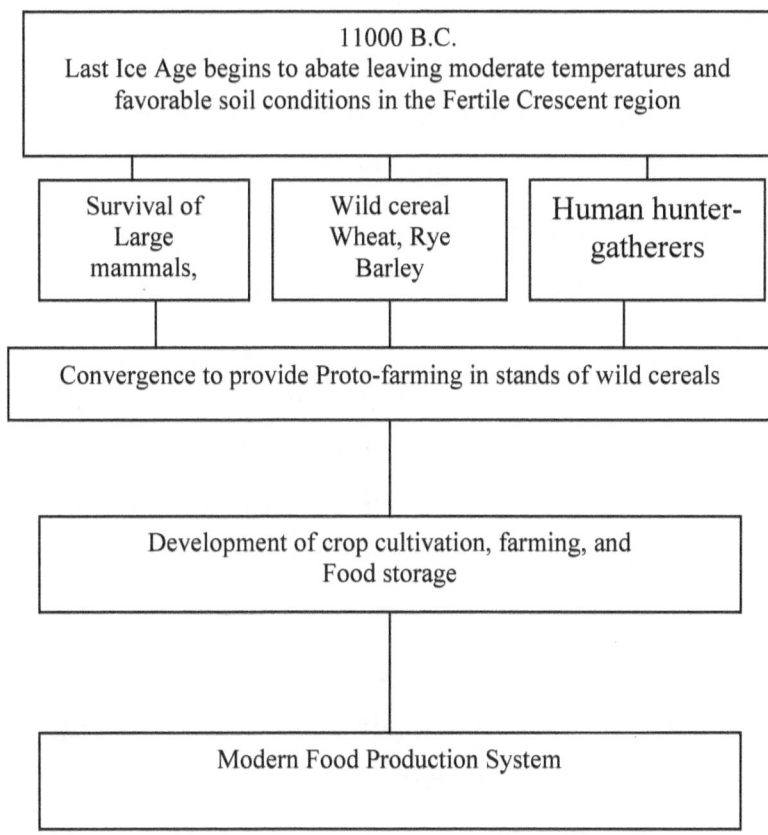

ARTHUR JACKSON

Over the last 40,000 years humans have developed a sophisticated system of food production. The components are reciprocally connected and are a group of independent but interrelated elements comprising a unified whole. The important thing to understand is that this system would fundamentally change the relationship between humans, plants, and other members of the animal kingdom. For the first time humans were making decisions as to which species would be selectively included in this system, and which would not. As humans moved from the last Ice Age into the current warming cycle, several factors came together in a synchronous matter which would enable this system to take hold and to become the important foundation system for human society it is today.

The first significant factor was the existence of stands of wild grains from seeds that had been moved over and over again during many hundreds of thousands of years by the advance and recession of glaciers. This process had acted as a transport system to create concentrations of wild grains in what is now known as the Fertile Crescent. One of the most important of these early cereals was barley. Although temperature sensitive, and seldom found above 1500 meters it has been found to be prevalent in and around early sites in habituated by humans (Harlan, 1966).These stands of wild grains offered a variety of foods for human hunter-gatherer's groups emerging from the last ice age. Along with the stands of grains came groups of animals hoping to share the readily available source of food in the region.

This was not unique to the Fertile Crescent and happened at several different locations all round the globe. China, India, and in North America habitants developed the technology of foraging these food sources. As we will see later in this text, all of the groups developed along common lines for many thousands of years. The important factor here is that animals, plants and the new emerging group of human hunter-gatherer's were converging at specific locations and interacting in a certain way to form the first embryonic Food Production System, farming.

These early systems were little more than human hunter gatherer groups being opportunistic. Finding readily available sources of wild grains, and the large numbers of animals attracted to the same food sources, these groups followed their natural instinct. When any species finds an available food source in a region, it will concentrate its efforts in that area until the food source is exhausted. In the case of humans they brought this natural instinct with them out of the last ice age, but also they brought changing social dynamics created over several generations and several cycles of glacial advance and decline. As humans began to localize their activities within these areas, there was no conscious thought about becoming sedentary, they were simply doing what all species do and stayed where there was available food in quantity, and with reliability throughout the yearly cycle.

Because of the location of these food sources it gives the appearance that early hunter gatherer groups were making a change in behavior from hunting and gathering, to the more sedentary pursuits of modern farming. Several of the earliest sites inhabited by early hunter gatherer groups appeared, at first glance to give support to this contention. However more recent studies have indicated that this was not the case. These groups remained in local areas because of the availability of food sources in substantial quantity and with a predictable reliability that encouraged them to remain within a certain area. These early communities were groups of up to 700 humans who inhabited areas of a few hundred acres (BELFER-COHEN, 1988). These groups resided in this location for a period of several generations doing little more than harvesting local wild grains that recurred on a yearly basis in the region. This repetitive activity kept them confined within an area of predictable and stable sources of food. In one of these locations humans even constructed walls around the fields of wild grain to protect this food source from all their competitors.

These sites were examples of humans not necessarily understanding the concept of farming, so much as being simply opportunistic and selecting areas which provided food for them with a minimal amount of effort on their part. It would take several generations before humans would begin to develop the concept of farming. Over several generations the system which developed around these activities began to focus on selecting certain types of grains as desirable, and excluding other types of plants as undesirable.

In many different parts of the world different plants serve as desirable food sources. In the Fertile Crescent and in parts of Europe the focus was on wheat, barley, and rye as desirable food sources. In China, the grain of choice was rice, while in the Americas it was corn. This was selective exclusion. The system evolving was changing the way humans perceived the world around them and moving them in the direction of selecting certain types of plants as desirable for their nutrition and excluding others.

Concurrently with this process humans were also making decisions about animal domestication. Certain animals were given preference in terms of their desirability to form relationships with early human hunter gatherer groups as they moved into this process of selecting certain plants and animals. This created a new system involving humans, plants, and animals. This new system altered the behavior of not only the plants that were selected, but changed the genetic makeup of the plants, animals, and the humans who became involved in this new system of food production. The fundamental relationship between the groups would be forever altered.

Food , Energy , and Water

Early Settlements

As identified in figure number one we can see the
development of stable food production from its modest
beginnings to a stable, complex, and fully functional system.
For most of the early years as humanity moved out of the
last ice age into a time of relative stability, food production
was nothing more than an extension of the early skills
developed as a hunter-gatherer. Agriculture, or farming, was
far on the horizon of human development. The early efforts
of human activity were opportunistic groups, taking
advantage of the organization of certain foodstuffs by the
movement of glaciers. As glaciers had retreated, and
advanced during alternate cycles throughout numerous ice
ages, populations of grains became located in certain
regions. We can engage in endless speculation about why
large quantities of these grains ended up in the Fertile
Crescent, but it would be little more than that, speculation.
The grains ended up in large concentrations in these areas
due to a number of factors. One such factor could be that
the leading edge of glacial advance ended in these regions
near the equatorial plane of the planet over repeated cycles.
As the glaciers retreated, large groups of seeds, held

ARTHUR JACKSON

dormant in the ice fields, would find fertile conditions for growth and expansion. Humans would be only one of the species to take advantage of this bounty. After surviving the last ice age, finding a region which provided a large and stable supply of food would be attractive to a large number of species. The human groups who wandered into these areas would find it difficult to leave. This would encourage the beginnings of a sedentary pattern, and a noticeable change in behavior. At this time we must consider the concept of synchronicity; groups of unrelated elements coming together at an opportune moment in time, to form a system. Humans, edible plants, and large groups of animals were located in a small geographical area. Each had developed some forms of behavior that had made it possible for them to survive. These survival traits were coming together in a setting that would make them attractive to each other. Plants, with their great genetic diversity, found this region to be amenable to many of the diverse species of grasses animals found edible. These grasses would thrive in this region. Next, large mammals, having survived the last glacial period, would find this stable source of food a lure, impossible to resist, and stay in the area. Of the species found in this area, are many of those that would later become the first to be domesticated by humans. They would have the ability to live in close proximity to species other than their own easily, be relatively sedentary, and provide a number of resources humans would need. Finally, there were humans, just beginning the journey toward farming. These groups of humans would not only be moving toward sedentary life styles, they would be just starting to explore the use of selected plants, and animals on a recurring basis. This process would not be completed in a short period of time, but would take several thousand years, before the fully functioning system would become ingrained in both the attitudes, and behaviors of humans. Each year as these grains would once again flourish under optimal growing conditions bands of humans would be repeatedly drawn to the area, and the readily available source of food. We must remember that a hunter gathering group would obtain most of its nutritional requirements from grain, nuts, and berries. As mentioned previously hunting was often a large scale enterprise that yielded little in the way of results. However, much of that was about to change as groups of other species would be attracted to the same areas as humans. This would also greatly increase the number of successful hunts. For the first time humans would find themselves not only with an abundance of grains, but with an easily acquired source of protein from other animals existing in close proximity to this ready supply of grains. It would take several thousand years before the system would become organized enough to become self sustaining, but it did occur. By the time we reach 9000 to 7000 B.C., we begin to see the emergence of increased group size and changes in organization and structure, which heralded the early arrival of human society. Two of the earliest examples of this were identified in the Middle East as Jericho, Catal Huyuk. These early settlements were some of the earliest examples of urban existence. Here humans exhibited changes in behavior that set them apart from their earlier hunter-gatherer's existence. There was evidence of occupational specialization and the early formation of social structure, political structure, and the creation of ruling groups around each of these settlements. There was also evidence of well-developed and well-structured craft activity such as metal working, creation of jewelry, and pottery used for storage. There is some indication of the emergence of art in the form of sculptures and paintings as well. These are all activities which can only proliferate and exist when a species has the luxury of additional time created by stable food sources. In this environment the early ingredients for a stable civilization would come together. Surpluses in food were sufficient to support the beginnings of the farming system. These centers appear to have engaged in trade as their populations began to grow. At their height, these settlements had populations of approximately 2000 to 6000 people living in a fixed geographical location and engaging in repetitive activity of cultivation of the grain sources. Although these groups were limited and isolated examples of the departure from hunter gathering, they marked a significant development in the human March toward social stability.

Each of these locations was near water sources, which is a fundamental requirement for stable food production based on grain collection. Jericho, was located along the Jordan River on a site that was over ten acres in size. The early humans in this settlement constructed domed homes of mud and brick, with floors. These windowless dwellings were accessible through a single frame entryway, or doorway. Many of the structures had as many as three rooms. An additional change that was brought about by this sedentary activity was the need to protect the grain sources and other food sources up on which the settlement would maintain its existence. In this settlement there was evidence of the construction of protective barriers in the form of a ditch and a wall around the settlement and its food sources. These constructions are particularly important for another reason. It marks one of the earliest time frames when humans also began the process of domestication of other animals. The structures would be necessary to keep such domesticated species in close proximity to humans.

Another example of early human settlements would be Catal Huyuk. The settlement occurred somewhat later in time than Jericho, and at its peak occupancy maintained a population of up to 6000 people. The housing construction was rectangular and was built of mud dried bricks. The dwellings had windows, chimneys, and fireplaces, and showed a remarkable similarity in construction, often recognized as a movement toward uniformity of construction. Each home was constructed in close proximity to its neighbor to provide a natural degree of fortification for the settlement. Each of the homes also had storage facilities for excess grains.

In just a few thousand years humanity would evolve from simple hunter-gatherers to a more sedentary creatures and collectors of naturally occurring grains stuffs. Even at this point humanity was not fully engaged in farming, but was opportunistic in its approach to naturally recurring foodstuffs. This process would stay in place for many thousands of years as humans increased in number, and as they recognized the potential benefit of collecting these grains and animal domestication. Figure 3 shows this new relationship, and Table 1 gives a perspective of human population growth during several time frames. As the table indicates, early human populations were small. But as the new system began to emerge, human population grew. The selection of certain species of plants and animals to be preferred, and to some degree controlled was a significant step in human evolution.

Human movement toward domestication shifted the relationship between these three groups. Initially, domestication of these wild grasses would be a larger factor in the stable food system emerging. Domestication of animals, while important would take many generations to accomplish. The diagram below illustrates this principal.

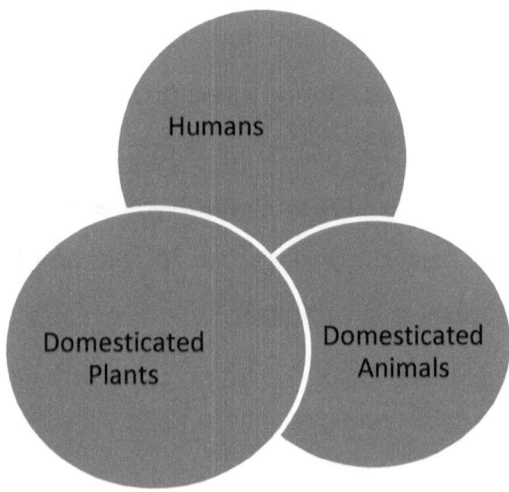

Figure 3 The system of Domestication

Food , Energy , and Water

Table 1 WORLD POPULATION, YEAR 0 TO NEAR STABILIZATION

Year	Population in Millions
0	.30
1000	.31
1250	.40
1500	.50
1750	.79
1800	.98
1850	1.26
1900	1.65
1910	1.75
1920	1.86
1930	2.07
1940	2.30
1950	2.52
1960	3.02
1970	3.70
1980	4.44
1990	5.27
1999	**5.98**
2000	6.06
2010	6.79
2020	7.50
2030	8.11
2040	8.58
2050	8.91
2100	9.46
2150	9.75
Near stabilization (after 2200)	Just above 10 billion

Source: United Nations Population Division.

Several of the species would become very important in the development of farming by humans, as pointed out by Harlan and Zohary and their 1996 article on the distribution of wild wheat and barley. Most important of these was barley which spread in abundance throughout the region known as the Fertile Crescent. At the end of the last ice age the availability of this and other grains would have a profound impact on the behavior of humans. Farming was a process that occurred during the interglacial periods, and that took hold as part of a system propelling humans forward in their evolution. It is clear that climate change had a significant impact on marine and vegetation zones which would have been compressed toward the equator, as the ice buildup took large amounts of usable moisture out of the atmosphere and locked it up in the ice caps. As Hewitt has pointed out, these rapid oscillations in climate would cause populations of plants and animals to pass through many adaptations and reorganizations in their genome and organizational structure. It would be necessary for species to move and adopt or become extinct in order to accommodate these changes. For humans this would come at a particularly important time, as recent studies have indicated that human populations would have been no more than 10,000 individuals in Africa during this period of the upper Pleistocene (Ambrose,

1998). This is identified as the time called a long genetic bottleneck in human evolution. This has also become part of a discussion about factors which drive the species toward extinction. An important question to consider at this juncture; whether humans were nearing the brink of extinction during the end of the last major glacial period?

ARTHUR JACKSON

What is extinction.

Although human populations had undergone an extreme degree of stress, and their numbers had been reduced to a population size globally of less than 10,000 individuals by many of the established studies, would this have placed Humanity on the road to extinction? As pointed out by Spiegelman" *most species are not driven to extinction before genetic factors impact them,* (Spielman, 2004), There is some controversy concerning the role of genetic factors in species extinction. His study conducted by looking at internationally established databases of threatened species found the issue of diversity as being a significant factor in a species movement toward extinction. He concluded that threatened species have populations that are in decline, which indicates a reduced reproductive fitness and elevated extinction risk. This was a change from the generally accepted hypothesis that most species are driven to extinction before genetic factors impact them. Lack of diversity was seen as a major factor leading toward biological extinction.

As humanity found itself in a genetic bottle neck, its declining population size would have been moving it rapidly toward extinction. Genetic factors become an important part in this process because species that have small or declining populations will often result in inbreeding and an overall loss of genetic diversity. There's a correlation between population size and loss of genetic diversity and inbreeding as defined by Richard Frankham in his 2005 paper, " Genetics and extinction" (Frankham, 2005). Once a species is reduced to inbreeding it reduces the diversity in reproductive populations and has a significant impact on survival. It will increase the risk toward extinction even where other factors are controlled. Humanity with a declining population moving out of the last global ice age would have found itself in such a situation.

These reductions in numbers are termed genetic bottle necks. The existence of a genetic bottle neck may be caused by several factors, such as epidemic disease, founder affects, global climate change, or volcanic winter just to name a few. The overall impact of a bottleneck is to reduce genetic diversity within a species. This reduction is a prime factor in moving an individual species closer to extinction. Several studies have been undertaken to resolve this growing conflict about the role of genetic factors in species extinction. In an earlier study, Ambrose correlated the impact of volcanic winner on human populations and their diversity. He discussed the potential impact of climate and geological factors, such as volcanic winter upon human population dispersal in relation to the

47

multiple dispersal models. He noted that additional bottlenecks may have occurred. Although his study was based upon the effect of volcanic activity, it demonstrated the significant impact on human populations of planetary forces. Human population could have been reduced to numbers of less than 40 breeding individuals for two centuries according to the study (Jones, 1986). Although this number would increase over time, human populations at some point would have been below 4000 individuals for a period of time in excess of 15,000 years over the surface of the entire planet. Numbers this small would have created a significant pressure moving humans closer to extinction. Other more recent studies have supported this as they have examined the impact of such genetic factors as extreme lack of diversity on the survival of species. One such study by was conducted by Spielman and Brook (Spielman, 2004). In this study they concluded that species that are threatened by extinction have a lower genetic diversity than non-threatened species and this is an indication of less reproductive fitness within a species. This lack of reproductive robustness would make it very difficult for any species to continue as a viable over long periods of geological time without succumbing to extinction.

At times humans would have a global population of less than 10,000. Although geological conditions in terms of food supplies, temperature, and habitable range for the species would have been stable, the overall impact on the species because of lack of diversity would have been a significant factor driving it toward extinction. The major problem is that small populations of any individual species do not have the flexibility to adapt to changing environmental or other factors. Environmental change is experienced by all species, and the need to cope with these changes is directly impacted when the species number is small. This would be a substantial hurdle facing humans as they emerged from the last glacial period. What would be the difference between humans and other threatened species in the situation?

ARTHUR JACKSON

The Unreasonable Human

The evolution of most species whether plant or animal is dependent upon that species' ability to adapt to changing environmental factors and genetic diversity. As food supply would increase, populations could increase in response. A subsequent decline in food would signal individual species to reduce their numbers to accommodate the smaller food supply. Likewise, with plants, an availability of fertile soil and hospitable climate and growing conditions would mark an expansion of all plants to accommodate these new favorable conditions. This was the process as seen between each period of glacial retreat. This is what can be called reasonable expectations for an individual species. Yet what happens if a species does not follow these reasonable expectations.

"A reasonable man adapts to his environment, while an unreasonable man insists that the environment adopt to fit him".

This is a paraphrase of a quote from- Oscar Wilde which most accurately describes the behavior of humans just prior to the younger dryas.

Food , Energy , and Water

Recent studies have indicated that the transition to agriculture among humans was far from being a linear process. The movement toward agriculture began around 15,000 years ago. This corresponds to the end of the last glacial period and a general warming trend and prolonged period of climate stability. This also marked a wetter period, with more free water available for plants and animals. An interesting study created in 2003 used the creation of a small game index as a measure of monitoring human development. The small game index measured foraging efficiency in and around human habitation sites and provided a measure of sight occupation intensity as defined by Munro in 2003. She put together information on the types of small game that could be cataloged at the individual sites. They used human foraging efficiency as a way of measuring the total energy gain for hunting after they had subtracted out the cost and efforts of capturing the game as a way of evaluating how efficient and capable the sites were. They expected see a direct correlation between the amounts of energy used to capture game and the activity in and around the individual sites. For instance, in the Mediterranean during this time some of the favorite types of small game were the spur-thigh tortoise, a range of waterfowl species, and the Cape hare. They ranked each of these types of game on a scale. The slow-moving target was easily captured and did not require special technology and is thus ranked very high. The waterfowl and the hare are fast-moving and require significantly more effort and more elaborate technologies and strategies such as nets, bows, arrows and traps for their capture. These particular types of small game would rank low on the index. As more and more of these low ranked animals, (hair, waterfowl) appeared in the record the index would drop, signaling a reduction in forging as humans began to invest more time in the capture of game to receive the same returns. It was interesting that they noted that haunting also exerted a significant pressure on the other animal populations. This was especially true for species that had a low turnover rate, or low fertility. They produced the table showing how this index could be applied to human activities starting at around 15,000 BP and moving forward to around 10,000 BP. That table is reproduced here in part:

SITE	CULTURAL PERIOD	TIME PERIOD (CAL B.P.)	SMALL GAME SAMPLE SIZE	REFERENCE
El-Wad Cave	Early Natufian	14,500-13,000	1092	Munro 2001
Hayonim Cave	Early Natufian	14,000-13,000	4728	Munro 2001
Hayonim Cave	Late Natufian	13,000-11,500	3279	Munro 2001
Hayonim Cave	Late Natufian	13,000-11,500	4226	Munro 2001
Hilazon Tachtit	Late Natufian	13,000-11,500	975	Munro 2001
Netiv Hagdud	PPNA	11,500-10,000	742	Tchernov `1994
Gilgal	PPNA	11,500-10,000	47	Noy et al 1980

Table 2 Cultural periods, time periods, and references for assemblages from the Levantine series.

ARTHUR JACKSON

Time ranges are provided for the general cultural period and are not given individually for each site. All dates *are in calibrated years BP* and taken from the paper *"Small game, the younger dryas, and the transition to agriculture in the southern levant",* (Munro, 2003)

This index indicates that these people put more energy into the capture of small game than previous populations of humans. However this does not indicate a point of irrevocable movement toward agriculture, instead it shows an abrupt interruption characterized by increased mobility of groups and reduced occupation at specific sites. This shows that the movement toward agriculture was not linear, but an irregular and often bumpy road because of the large variety in packs of humans and demography of settlement types and mobility. Use of this index has made it possible for us to understand that agriculture was not the preferred method for humans during times when climate was favorable. In fact, during the last interglacial period humans may have tested farming, or enhanced foraging techniques, only to abandon them. In fact recent evidence would show that farming became a constant and stable source of human endeavors only after the younger dryas with its resultant change in climate and temperature.

While in a more favorable climate, farming did not predominate. This study is interesting for another reason. It is the first to correlate food production to energy balance directly. No matter what system we examine, the need to gain more energy than you expend is critical, if the system is to survive. Although farming would change the relationship between humans and the environment for ever, it was a system that required significant energy input. Ultimately, the need to cultivate specific crops at the expense of others is a key step in developing farming.

Cultivation, which is a necessary strategy to increase yields may have been preceded by several periods of experimentation and subsequently abandoned. There's growing evidence that cultivation, the domestication of crop plants and man existed in close association with humans in the past 7000-100000 years. Another interesting study involving linkage disequilibrium (non random Association of alleles) focused on the recent results in Maize and other plant species and their parallels with human data. These domesticated plants have existed alongside human populations and therefore some population size related effects might not be entirely independent. It is of interest to note that the domestication process can be seen as a type of genetic bottle neck but is not random and is associated with human selection of specific types of plants. I referred to this earlier as selective exclusion in preference to a more desirable type of plant or animal. As humans became more entrenched in the process of cultivation and domestication, they were intentionally removing species of plants and animals in an effort to make geography more sustainable to specific desirable types of plants and animals. Domestication is a process that reduces diversity in a species, and in the species they impact.

The domestication of plants and the breeding of domestic species of animals is a breeding bottle neck that leads to a pronounced decrease in diversity. Humans had made an unreasonable choice in deciding to move toward farming and away from hunter gathering, or enhanced hunter gathering practices. There are still tribes in the modern world that utilize enhanced Hunter gathering techniques. Tribes located in New Guinea often will employ these techniques in establishing fields of produce that they will plant, leave, and come back to at some later date as their group moved back through the area. This requires some sort of preparation, and rudimentary skills in developing and protecting the young plants. However, these groups are not sedentary and will often continue movement to other areas leaving these crops to develop in large part on their own. The distinction between these groups and farming is that farmers stay on site to protect and develop a food source. Along with this domestication of plants comes the inevitable domestication of animals as an augment to food supply. This would also require a selective inclusion of specific types of animals that would be more favorable to domestication. This was first investigated by Konrad Lorenz a Pioneer in animal behavior. He identified several of the characteristics that would be necessary to find particular types of animals suitable for domestication. This will often mean creating some type of imprint between humans and the animals while in their juvenile state.

A similar process would be used in determining plant domestication. Although we do not usually think of plants as having the ability to imprint, we do recognize that certain plants were more desirable because of their yield characteristics than others. In both cases, the need was to determine the species that had the required social characteristics that were beneficial to humans. For the first time, humanity was making a conscious decision between a adjusting to the environment, and adjusting the environment to their needs. We often do not make this correlation between social characteristics and plants and animals. Yet, each species of plant suitable for domestication exhibited a certain behavior in its growth pattern which made it suitable, in a social sense, to the needs of humanity. Likewise as we look at the number of animals that were domesticated and their social characteristics we see distinct correlation as indicated in the following table:

Domestication   **Table**

Animal	Where Domesticated	Date
Dog	East Asia	13,000 BC
Sheep	Western Asia	8500 BC
Cat	Fertile Crescent	8500 BC
Goats	Western Asia	8000 BC
Pigs	Western Asia	7000 BC
Cattle	Eastern Sahara	7000 BC
Guinea pig	Peru	6000 BC
Chicken	Thailand	6000 BC
Horse	Kazakhstan	3600 BC
Silkworm	China	3500 BC
Llama	Peru	3500 BC
Ass	Egypt	3000 BC
Dromedary camel	Saudi Arabia	3000 BC
Honey Bee	Egypt	3000 BC
Duck	Western Asia	2500 BC
Yak	Tibet	2500 BC
Goose	Germany	1500 BC
Alpaca	Peru	1500 BC
Reindeer	Siberia	1000 BC

Table 3 commonly accepted dates of animal domestication for selected species. Periods for each animal type are approximate. Taken from "The Archeology of Animals, by Simon Davis.

Along with each species of animal identified in table 3 for its social characteristics and domesticated, there were corresponding plants that underwent the same process. The individual plants that were chosen for domestication, must provide similar characteristics to those of domesticated animals. They must provide a substantial yield benefit in terms of energy input to energy received something that hunting of small game would not necessarily provide. They must yield to domestication easily. They must be amenable to transport and translocation over a significant geographical area, thus meeting the requirements of social compatibility. In the following table we will see species of plants that satisfied these characteristics.

Plant	Where Domesticated	Date
Fig trees	Near East	9000 BC
Rice	East Asia	9000 BC
Barley	Near East	8500 BC
Einkorn wheat	Near East	8500 BC
Emmer wheat	Near East	8500 BC
Chickpea	Anatolia	8500 BC
Bottle gourd	Central America	8000 BC
Maize	Central America	7000 BC
Broomcorn millet	East Asia	6000 BC
Bread wheat	Near East	6000 BC
Manioc/Cassava	South America	6000 BC
Potato	South America	5000 BC
Avocado	Central America	5000 BC
Chili peppers	South America	4000 BC
Watermelon	Near East	4000 BC
Pomegranate	Iran	3500 BC
Hemp	East Asia	3500 BC
Sunflower	Central America	2600 BC
Sweet Potato	Peru	2500 BC
Sorghum	Africa	2000 BC
Sunflower	North America	2000 BC
Pearl millet	Africa	1800 BC
Chocolate	Mexico	1600 BC
Chenopodium	North America	750 BC

Table 4   Plant Domestication Table of Dates and Places

By   K.   Kris   Hirst,   About.com   Guide,
http://archaeology.about.com/od/domestications/a/pla
nt_domestic.htm

Domestication did not mean humanity became absolutely fixed in place, but would create the need to bring species into areas where they would not normally be located. Once farming had taken hold, humanity would transport its food sources with the group whenever they moved. This is often supported by the fossil record where we begin to see animal species not indigenous to an area and plants not indigenous to an area begin to appear in new areas. This process will often mean dislocating and removing indigenous animals and plant species to accommodate human needs. Humanity was in the process of changing its environment rather than adapting to the environment. Along with these changes came other changes including morphological change, size differences, species frequency change within a succession of groups, and other cultural factors, such as sex and age related culling of species would be indicated. These factors would be consistent for both plants and animals. In order to protect these newly developed resources humans would have to devise schemes to protect them from predators. For plants that would be the need to create protective geographical areas that could be guarded against other plants and animals. Although we do not think of this as herding to any large extent, it is essentially that. Plants were grouped in a protected area where they could be monitored and guarded. Likewise the same process would be used for animals. Once again we must take a look at the Energy relationship of these types of endeavors.

As stated in his book, " The Archeology of Animals", Davis 1984, the following relationship between energy utilized and energy received in the move from hunting and gathering to early farming was made;

> "For a long time it was believed that the transition from hunting to husbandry was a move from a precarious existence to one providing assured sustenance. The idea that hunting and gathering required high expenditure of energy with little return ... and that a major labor saving is obtained by a switch to farming is probably wrong. Richard Lee (1968), studied the !Kung bushmen, hunter-gatherer's in the Kalahari of southern Africa. He discovered that bushmen en joy plentiful and balanced diet and only spend an average of 2.5 days per week in their quest for food. Similarly, Australian

aboriginal in Arnhem Land spend an average of 3.5 to 5 hours per day food gathering and this activity is not particularly arduous. It is now "realized that farming and husbanding animals are much more difficult than hunting and gathering and require a higher input of labor. "

The archeology of Animals", Davis 1984, page 152

Farming was indeed a high energy input endeavor. Yet the transition to farming and domestication of plants and animals was a necessary step in order for humanity to avoid the inevitable consequences of possible extinction. This relationship would forever mark the changes between humanity and its environment. Whether it was the extreme temperature changes of the younger dryas that interrupted the warming interglacial period, or if it was population pressure and cultural/economic changes that caused humans to move to farming and domestication the results were no less pronounced. At that point a given area of land would support a larger number of people with farming and domestication of plants and animals. However this benefit did not come without cost. Thomas Malthus an economist from the 17th century first identified population levels as being dependent on the availability of food sources rather than population pressure directly stimulating economic change. The Malthus Effect would have a profound impact on human evolution as we moved from rudimentary farming and domestication to more sophisticated social structures.

The Malthus effect

Despite its adoption of farming and the resultant domestication of plants and animals, humanity was only slightly removed from the other species that surrounded it in nature. Although this new technology, farming and domestication, would provide stable food sources, the energy balance between input to the system and the resultant output of energy was not overly significant. Although humans could provide stable food sources under most conditions, there were still circumstances that would make the production of food through farming, and the domestication of plants and animals difficult. Climate factors such as rain, drought, or cold were still considerations that would affect the yield. Likewise there was always the problem of insects, disease, and the lack of proper chemical balance in the soil to affect energy transfer that was required. Humanity with its new technology was simply a half step away from their brothers and sisters who remained hunter-gatherers. Although the process was beneficial, human populations increased on a par with other animal populations for many thousands of years. Before we reach the 1800's, the time of Malthus, the distinction between human economies and those of other animals and plants was minimal. Malthus wrote to this fact in appreciation of this lack of distinction between humans and other animals ;

> 'I say, that the power of population is indefinitely greater than the power in the earth to produce subsistence for man. Population, when unchecked, increases in a geometrical ratio. Subsistence increases only in an arithmetical ratio. A slight acquaintance with numbers will shew the immensity of the first power in comparison of the second.
>
> By that law of our nature which makes food necessary to the life of man, the effects of these two unequal powers must be kept equal.
>
> This implies a strong and constantly operating check on population from the difficulty of subsistence. This difficulty must fall somewhere and must necessarily be severely felt by a large portion of mankind. "

Thomas Malthus, An Essay on the Principle of Population, 1798, AN ESSAY ON THE PRINCIPLE OF POPULATION, AS IT AFFECTS THE FUTURE IMPROVEMENT OF SOCIETY WITH REMARKS ON THE SPECULATIONS OF MR. GODWIN, M. NDORCET, AND OTHER WRITERS.LONDON, PRINTED FOR J. JOHNSON, IN ST. PAUL'S CHURCH-YARD, 1798.

Food , Energy , and Water

Despite over 10,000 years of technological development in farming and domestication, development of cities and social structure, humanity was still tied to the same rules that govern most other species in nature. Gregory Clark fully explored the Malthus effect on human societies in his ground breaking work, "A Farewell to Alms", Princeton University Press 2007. Clark made the clear connection between the quality of human habitat and the resultant productivity were still depended on birth and death rates and a range of environmental, cultural and other factors. Although population density had increased significantly, due to the increase in technological development in farming techniques and in cultivation, and the rise of social systems, such as the rise of stable governments, humanity was still very closely tied to other species in its search for survival. Although agriculture, and domestication were adopted because they were initially better technological models which generated higher productivity per area of land mass, as populations grew, this inevitably lead to a decrease in living standards as societies worked to reach a new equilibrium under the Malthus model. Human populations grew very gradually until we reach the early 1400s.

Under this model, the average person in the 1800's was no better off than the person of 100,000 B.C. As the quality of life tended to be spread over larger growing populations it resulted in an overall equilibrium in standards of living which did not improve. Although new technologies such as farming provided greater productivity for humanity, resulting population growth absorbed that productivity and tended to spread it over the populations resulting in only minimal gains in the standard of living for each individual. This is what is known as the Malthus trap. Every successful group in of society whose production greatly outstripped the needs of the individual group, that access tended to be redistributed over other segments of the population who were far less productive. The result was a general but minimal increase in living standards for the overall society. This concept of wealth is how we define the success of societies in the modern world. Table 5 shows the correlation between Technology and population over the last 10000 years, and Figure 4, shows how population was affected throughout time.

Figure 4 Human Population Growth over time

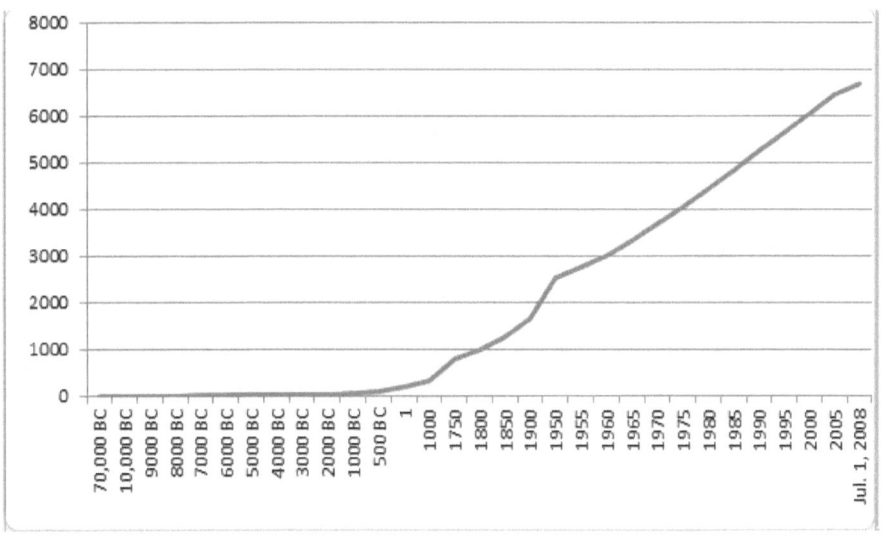

Table 5 Technological impacts on Population

World Population Growth 1804-1992

>1 billion 1804
>
>2 billion 1927 (123 years later)
>
>3 billion 1960 (33 years later)
>
>4 billion 1974 (14 years later)
>
>5 billion in 1987 (13 years later)

Source Data Book 1999

1800 marks the age of industrialization

1927 marks the age of electricity

1960 marks the age of the transistor

1974 marks the age of the personal computers

1987 marks the age of the internet and mobile communications

As humanity shifted to this new paradigm, technology, there was an increase in food production and an eventual stability of food supply. However, this shift did not provide humanity with anything more than a marginal increase in stability. Populations tended to grow slowly as food supplies were increased marginally due to the multiplying effect of farming. Farming and the associated technologies are nothing more than the ability of an individual to multiply their individual impact on a given area of land. From about 10,000 BP until the recent past, human food production was dependent upon manpower to select cultivated seeds, protect those seeds, and reap the energy transfer resultant from cultivation for the individual. As Humanity moved into the domestication of animals, we begin to see the first impact of a multiplier effect. With the cultivation of domesticated species for heavy labor, we begin to see that in individual can have a more pronounced impact on the productive entity of a given parcel of land. Prior to domestication large numbers of people will required to be able to utilize cultivation techniques and to benefit from those techniques. In many of the early settlements hundreds of individuals were often be necessary to utilize the productive increase from a small number of acres. These numbers were not necessary for a single short period of time, they would be necessary for the entire growing cycle of the selected plants. As we can see in many modern-day hunter gatherers' societies' preparation of the site and its protection is manpower intensive. A rough figure of merit for manpower utilization prior to the domestication of animals was roughly 100 humans per acre. These early stage farms were little more than humans gathering selected grasses for consumption. The process of cultivation over many hundreds of years led to an eventual organizational structure with clusters of humans developing farming technology for collective effort.

Although the shift in human behavior, in adopting new technology had successfully moved Humanity from the brink of extinction, it set the species on a road that was markedly different from the rest of the animals and plants. In order for these fledgling farmers to be successful, groups of plants and animals had to be systematically excluded from the environment in a process that continues to be seen today in many of our endeavors. This exclusion is necessary to protect the preferred sources of plants and animals from predators, whether, and any other unforeseen events. These early settlements were marginally efficient, but sufficient to stabilize food sources and to allow human populations to begin a long-term sustainable growth in numbers. Starting about 7000 BP

Humanity moved forward with another technological advancement in the creation of pottery, which allowed storage of these grains and to some degree of domesticated animal carcasses for long periods of time. We begin to see at this point in time the establishment of large stable prominent collections of humans. In the Middle East, such names as Jericho, and Kfar were some of the first large settlements based upon domestication of plants and animals. We also begin to see at this point in time the emergence of architecture and the use of engineering building materials, such as plasters being used. The structures represent a more significant shift away from hunter-gatherer's and toward full farming and domestication of plants and animals. The new requirements to maintain these facilities were significant, however the benefit in energy surplus obtained from these enclaves provided a marginal increase to the overall groups. And more importantly these marginal increases were sustainable and reproducible year after year. Despite this, humanity was still in the grips of the Malthus trap. Food production would still be the governing factor in population growth. The more people available for labor, the larger the food supply, but this increase was then spread over the increased number of people necessary to produce the food. This acted as a regulator on human growth keeping it sustained and slow.

Food , Energy , and Water

Here we must consider factors in the driving force moving humanity toward more technological change. In the Malthus trap, food supply continued to create equilibrium between population growth and stability, although other factors would begin to play a part in this development. Available sources of land, climate, and the ultimate conflict between members of the species for these limited resources would become significant factors in determining how Humanity would expand from this point. Starting around 4000 BP, humanity began to engage in domestication of animals. It was at this time European society began the domestication of large work animals, such as horses, Oxon, cattle, and other large animals capable of doing work for humans that we begin to see a multiplier effect have some significant impact on human production of food.

It is at this point in time that we begin to see humans move away from and out of the Malthus trap. With large-scale domestication of working animals, humans were able to reduce the manpower required per unit of land in order for it to be productive. It also became possible for small groups of humans to have a more significant impact on the ecology around them. This small step in utilizing domesticated animals had provided a nudge to humanity on the road to technologically sustainable food independence. With the use of such animals not only for labor, but for transportation, human organizations could have a larger footprint than their predecessors. It was possible during these times for individual groups, with high productivity, to produce substantial amounts of surplus. This surplus was often the key to creating the beginnings of trade between groups. Trade became a significant factor in furthering human advancement and establishing human systems necessary for organize an orderly society. It also marked a point in human evolution when society could afford to tolerate and to support members that were not necessarily productive in generating food. In most hunter-gatherer societies every member of the group must provide some degree of energy toward the creation of food for the group. We were beginning to see humans able to allocate time toward non food producing activities. The emergence of artisans, craftsman, and other groups that did not provide directly to the transfer of energy to the group in terms of food production began to emerge. Despite these modest gains, humanity was still not fully removed from the Malthus trap.

The first true break between human societies and the constraints of nature as proposed by the Malthus trap, came during the 14th through the 18th century. This was the emergence of the Industrial Revolution, a period of time that would forever alter the relationship between humanity and nature. Where animal domestication had provided a marginal increase in productivity for humanity, the measure of the society success was still its ability to be able to feed its people, and the resulting impact of food supplies on birth rates and population stability. But although they had been marginal increases as result of farming, and domestication, humanity was still tied to slow, but stable population growth related to the food cycle.

This would also be true for other geographical areas. China was keeping pace with Europe in agricultural productivity well into 1700s. Chinese agriculture and productivity was comparable to much of Europe. As indicated in Table 6. Figures from the 1600-1800s showed a parity in efficiency between these two regions. Both cultures were using manpower and animal power in most areas of the work to achieve greater efficiency.

ARTHUR JACKSON

Table 6 Comparisons of Income per Day

	English Midlands Pence	Yangtze Delta Copper cash	Yangtze Delta Pence
man, per day worked	22 d	229 cash	30.5 d
man averaged over year	17 d	115 cash	15 d
woman, per day worked	11-14	58 cash	8 d
Family Average over a year	20 d	140 cash	19 d

Agricultural Productivity Comparisons

	English Midlands C. 1806	Yangtze Delta C. 1620	Yangtze Delta C. 1820

Food , Energy , and Water

output(£)/acre	3.30	24.45	27.35
days per acre	13.0	111.8	127.7
output (d)/day	60.9	52.5	51.4

Yangtze output values were all in c. 1820 cash
prices and were
converted to pence by dividing by the PPP
exchange rate

From: *"Agricultural Productivity and Rural Incomes in England and the Yangtze Delta"*, c. 1620- c. 1820, by Robert C. Allen, Nuffield College New Road, Oxford OX1 1NF, United Kingdom

The industrial revolution would forever alter that dynamic. The industrial revolution marked a rapid and abrupt departure from the constraints of conventional nature, and the move into a new and challenging world for humanity. It would also mark the divergence of Europe from other societies in overall efficiency.

Starting in the 1400's we see the emergence of new technologies that enabled societies to have a more significant impact per unit of land than at any other time in the past. Early farming societies were hugely dependent upon large numbers of people in order to make land productive. Even with the advent of animal domestication the multiplier effect obtained was minimal. Instead of requiring several hundred people per acre of land to make it productive, with the use of domesticated animals we could now have an average of four to five people per acre to make an acre of land productive. We begin to see the first movement away from this process in England, which is largely credited with being the birthplace of the industrial revolution.

However this did not occur without sufficient preparation. In the early 12th century much of England was still an agrarian and feudal society. Between 1200 to 1400 BP, English society was undergoing a dramatic transformation. Feudal lords, which had relied heavily upon the manpower of tenant farmers to provide surplus food and material, were now moving away from that paradigm. Large numbers of individuals were being forced off of what were termed as common areas around feudal estates. These common areas were large tracts of land that were used by individuals for farming and subsistence. The land was not actually owned by the individual, but which utilize by families and groups of families for many generations. As societies became more organized, with the establishment of a strong central government, there was a need to provide revenue for the government so that it might function. In order to do this the government taxed land owned by individuals. Since these common areas were not technically only by the people who resided there, the land was reclaimed by the government and the individual forced off the land which was then sold to recognize and identify individuals that could be taxed. As large numbers of people were forced from the land, their only recourse was to move into cities where they could hope to find employment. However this large pool of cheap labor became a drain upon governments. It is not until the emergence of industrialization, by which we mean the large-scale use of mechanized devices for the production of goods and services, that this huge pool of contact labor became a resource rather than a liability. This change to mechanization also impacted food production. For the first time a single individual utilizing mechanization could control and effectively produce from dozens of acres of land. The advent of large-scale farming and ranching was coming into existence. In many places in England, it was not unusual for a single individual to own many hundreds of acres of land, while employing only a handful of people to maintain and to make the land productive. Mechanization made it possible to greatly expand control over and transportation of products produced over large geographical areas feasible, and economically desirable. Most of this product was food. Of the amount of product transported at the beginning of the industrial revolution, fully 70% was foodstuffs.

The Evolution of a Technology

Food and its production has been a central pillar of human society for many thousands of years. From the earliest periods of simple foraging, to the more complex periods of large-scale farming, the production of food has been essential. It represents not only advances in agriculture, but the first stable and long-term system of technological advancement for humanity. The evolution of agriculture is the evolution of technology. From the 14th century to the 18th century it would have a profound impact on human population growth.

The 14th to 18th century, a period of time loosely recognized as the renaissance, was a time rich in technological development. Farming in Europe had reached a point of near maximum efficiency based upon human Manpower, and domesticated animal power. Humanity had been engaged in a gradual but very steady increase in population until the beginning of the 14th century because of the stable and increased food supply. It was in fact the most stable, and the first, system of technology. Humanity had mastered selective exclusion among plants and animals to provide food supplies that were tailored to the specifics of human need and its growing society. Farmers produced food in abundance. Societies within Europe were beginning to engage in the earliest stages of true International Commerce. Food production was the first form of human capital, and would continue to play an important part in humanities future. The development of this technology provides us with an important window into the true capital of human society. It was during this time period that Europe began to diverge from other cultures in its farming efficiency, and in the development of technologies.

In the 14th century Europe was different from the other major areas of humanity in several very important ways. Although populations in China, India, and based upon new findings even in the Americas, were on a par with those of Europe, it was during this time that European Technology took a commanding lead over these cultures. China, India, and the Americas were very similar in their makeup. They were very large geographical areas, isolated from much of the rest of humanity by culture, and distance, while sharing homogenous populations, unifying governments, or religions. China had been unified for many years. India was governed by a succession of dominant governments, although lacking a unifying stable government, and was unified by a single dominant religion. The Americas were likewise situated, with the presence of large and unifying political units which governed large sections of the continent, according to more recent findings. Europe on the other hand was not a unified whole, but a system of individual states constantly vying with each other for dominance. This competition was vital to the spread of technology, the principle capital of humanity during the time frame. As societies grew more complex, Europe as independent states competing with each other, forced the exchange of technology and a growth of technology that we would not see in the other developing areas of humanity for many centuries.

This principle was first stated by a Canadian economist in the nineteen fifties. His name was Robert Mundell. Mundell was working for the Canadian government as that government was facing problems that would eventually begin to impact the rest of the world. The economy of Canada was tied closely to United States, its southern neighbor, and the dominant world power. Across the border between the two countries was a flow of technology and commerce. In such situations each country wants to create a stable relationship that will work to its benefit. In the case of Canada, it wanted to create a stable relationship with the United States, but could not find the method to do so. This was similar to the problems existing within Europe as stable nations worked to develop relationships with their neighbors that would allow them to create stability and permanence for themselves. Mundell recognized this phenomenon as a problem that was typical for all countries with open borders. Although he applied this theory to capital, it applies equally to technology in general. Competing societies must choose between two distinct paths in order to have stability with their neighbors. They may choose a path of independence, which ultimately leads to isolation and a termination of technology and commercial exchange with its neighbors. Or, they may choose another path in which they actively seek the exchange of technology and the stabilization of an exchange rate of technology between itself and its neighbors. In countries outside of Europe the former would dominate. Those societies pursued a path of independence, and resultant isolation which diminished the flow of information and technology, between them and other countries. Until we reached the 12th century BP, China had active trade with countries in Africa and Asia. It had a large and stable fleet which promoted trade and exploration and exchange between many different countries. After the 12th century China closed its borders and its fleet disappeared. There are a number of theories as to why this occurred, but it did happen. China became a closed society along with much of the rest of Asia for centuries. Likewise India was isolated by geography from much of the rest of the world, with little exchange of technology. In the Americas, although recent findings have indicated that there was a vibrant and very sophisticated civilization, it was dominated by small groups of empires. While creating uniformity and control of the populations, there was little exchange of technology with other regions because of its geographical isolation. Each of these areas had parity with Europe in terms of farming technology and food production efficiency until the beginning of industrialization. As Europe move toward industrialization and a different type of efficiency in food production and in other technologies it began to advance. These societies were dependent. Europe because of the close proximity of many stable states moved along a path of mobility of technology, with the resultant stable exchange of technology between nations. It was this concept that helped promote the initial surge of technology in 14th century Europe; that period of time that we recognized as the industrial revolution. This is the same rule that would ultimately force nations in two patterns of international trade in the centuries to follow.

The European countries would eventually evolve into a network, which would provide an exchange of information and technology crucial for continued advancement. It is this same process that we see today in the modern global community. In order for countries to succeed they must accept technological and commercial mobility, and develop some stable rate of exchange between themselves and the rest of the international community. Those countries which seek a path of independence, and its resultant isolationism will fall behind in terms of technology. This is largely why in the 16th through the 18th century we begin to see a massive divergence between productive efficiency in food production in Europe and the rest of the world. This also coincides with the emergence of other technologies in Europe. This simple rule would govern the development of all technologies, including the central technology of food production. A nation could be independent, or it could have mobile technology, with a stable exchange rate of technology, but not all three.

Food production, as the first and dominant form of technology had moved humanity from the brink of extinction, and helped to evade the Malthus trap. But, in pursuing this technology humanity had engaged in a process of selectively excluding large numbers of species in favor of a limited number of species that were beneficial to humanity. In both plants and animals this was the process of domestication. Although there are no accurate figures over the number of plant species that have been lost over these many thousands of years, recent data has been collected on species in use by humans.

Having created a compromise of sorts with nature, the growth of human populations was no longer dependent upon food supplies. For most other species, food supply is the governing factor for population growth. An abundant food source would be essential for species to increase its population. Likewise, a declining food supply would result in a corresponding decrease in population densities. Humanity with the aid of the technology had reduced this limiting factor. Human population began a steady and rapid growth, starting in the 14th century, with a resultant spike in population density in the 18th and 19th century. However, this did not solve the problem entirely. Human populations were increasing faster than technology could be applied to increase food sources.

The late 18th through the 19th century again saw population growth began to outstrip food supply. Food shortages were a common occurrence in many parts of the world. The basic tenets of technology, mechanization, although available in the late 18th century in Europe, did not find favor in much of the rest of the world until after World War Two. The tractor, while the principal implement allowing European and American farmers to leverage technological efficiency, and thus greatly increase food production did not find global application until after World War Two. That is when it was first applied to farming throughout Asia.

The existing model of farming until this point in time was that of the family farm. Increases in output where obtained largely with applications of domesticated animals and additional manpower. This model began to lose ground to growing food requirements in the middle of the 18th century. As more manpower and animal power were added to increase production, much of the increase in production was consumed by be additional work force. As human populations began to approach the 1 billion mark, maintaining substantial growth in food production by adding additional animals and humans to the work force was becoming impossible. The divergence at this time of European societies away from the use of additional manpower, and toward the use of mechanization as a vehicle for increasing food production, was the difference between success of European farming, and ultimately American farming, over the models employed in China, India, and the early Americans. Mechanization made it possible for individuals to develop large tracts of land with miniscule amounts of Manpower. Technology, as a multiplier, increased the food production output to a level that allowed population growth to continue. Yet, even this change would not sustain the necessary growth in food production an increasing human population would need. It would take an additional application of technology to provide the needed spark in output to sustain growing human populations. This change would not occur until after World War Two, and would not be the result of mechanization, but a new application of technology, plant modification, and new types of fertilizers.

In the 1940's food production in much of South America, Africa, and in many parts of Asia would lag far behind what was needed to maintain populations. Famines and food shortages were common. In an effort to address this problem a young microbiologist from the DuPont Co. accepted an appointment as a geneticist and a plant pathologist with an organization in Mexico to engage in scientific research on plant breeding, soil science and agronomy. Norman Borlaug working as part of a joint effort between the Rockefeller Foundation and the Mexican government began work on resolving the problem of hunger. As a result of his effort, new varieties of high-yielding disease resistant wheat were developed. For his effort Mr. Borlaug was awarded a Nobel Prize, and humanity had found the vehicle to increase food production in a very new and different way. Now, it was hoped humanity would finally be free of the cycle of starvation and famine. It would mark the beginning of many new varieties of plants, and eventually animals that humanity would use to continue boosting food production to stay ahead of its growing population. It would also mean the exclusion of many species.

In the long march of human history we have used approximately 100,000 plant species on a regular ongoing basis. As we have continued down the road of technology in developing our food system, we have excluded many other species. In today's world 95% of the food needs for humanity are met by less than 40 plant species. For animals as a domesticated food source, of the 50,000 species in the world today, only about 40, including both mammals and birds are used as domesticated species for food.

In Table 7 we can see how pronounced this process has been.

Food , Energy , and Water

Author	Year	No. of species	Uses
Heywood	1991	100,000	Used plants
Paroda and Mal	1993	80,000	Explored by humans since dawn of civilization
Myers	1983	75,000	Edible
Wilson	1992	30,000	Edible
Kunkel	1984	12,650	Edible
Uphof	1968	9,500	Economic uses
Wilson	1992	7,000	Source of food (wild/cultivated)
Terrell *et al.*	1977	3,000	Vascular species of economic importance
Zeven and de Wet	1982	2,489	Cultivated species excluding ornamentals, timber crops, and lower plants
Rehm	1994	2,454	Agronomic plants

Table 7 from Padulosi, S., Hodgkin, T., Williams J.T., and Haq International, N; *Estimates of number of plant species used around the world*, Plant Genetic Resources Institute (IPGRI), Rome, Italy; International Centre for Underutilized Crops (ICUC), Southampton, UK

Utilizing this small number of plants humanity made food production stay ahead of human population from 1960 to the present through the use of technology, and it has managed to stay marginally ahead of population growth, until the 1990s, when it began to decline again. With the application of modern farming and its use of plant modification and genetic manipulation, human populations remained severed from food. Indeed, population was now a driving force to cause increased food production, as shown in figure 5 and table 8.

Food , Energy , and Water

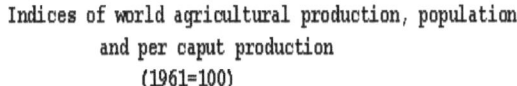

Indices of world agricultural production, population
and per caput production
(1961=100)

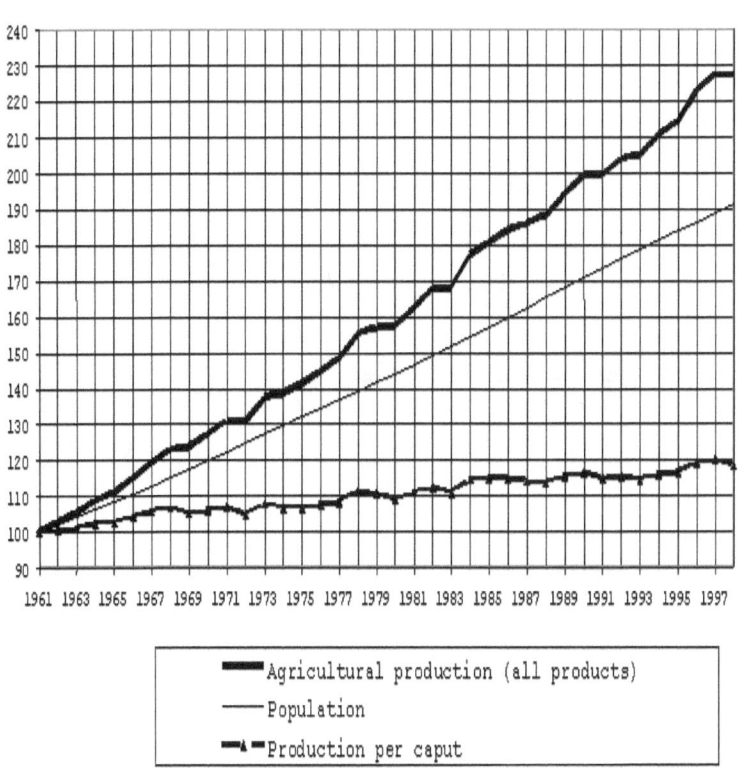

Figure 5-from, FAO SYMPOSIUM ON *AGRICULTURE, TRADE
AND FOOD SECURITY: ISSUES AND OPTIONS IN THE FORTHCOMING
WTO NEGOTIATIONS FROM THE PERSPECTIVE OF DEVELOPING
COUNTRIES,* Geneva, 23-24 September 1999

The trend in food production is shown in Table 9 below for several decades.

Table 8-World Growth in Agricultural Production and Demand1978-1997
(IN PERCENT PER YEAR)

	1978-1979		1988-1989		1998-1999	
	Production	Demand	Production	Demand	Production	Demand
All Commodities	2.28	2.20	2.13	2.09	1.97	1.91
Basic Food Stuffs	2.25	2.10	2.03	2.00	1.54	1.47

Table 8-Reproduced with data from; FAO SYMPOSIUM ON *AGRICULTURE, TRADE AND FOOD SECURITY: ISSUES AND OPTIONS IN THE FORTHCOMING WTO NEGOTIATIONS* Geneva, 23-24 September 1999

As we have grown more efficient in producing food, we have grown extremely selective in the species that we use. Despite this small number of species utilized, food production occupies 40% of all human endeavors. Maps revealing the extent to which food production dominates human enterprise have been compiled. It is the single largest endeavor of humanity, and it is based upon a handful of plants and animals. Although we have reduced the number of plants and animal species that we rely upon, we have increased the complexity through the use of genetics to satisfy the ever growing needs of human populations. In today's world farmers and ranchers face increasing demand from the marketplace which determines which species will be selected for production and which will be excluded. Marketplace changes will often shape the characteristics of individual species based on market place desires, and rule out thousands of other species as undesirable. With growing populations, there is ever increasing pressure to produce food products which meet the demanding and specific requirements of global populations. Whereas in nature species survive by having large and diverse populations, in the human model, diversity is confined to a small number of species.

ARTHUR JACKSON

Modern Farming

Modern farming has transformed human society in many new and unexpected ways. The system of food production itself is not without transformation. In a reversal of roles, human populations are no longer governed by food production, but food production is governed by the pressure of human population growth. As demonstrated in figure 6 and table 9 we can see that growth in human populations have resulted in transformations in food production to increase efficiency and to accommodate human needs. But more recently, with the creation of genetically engineered products, and modern fertilizers, the system of food production and the associated technologies have undergone even more rapid transformation. In today's world food production is not only driven by population needs, but by population desires. This behavior is not unusual and has many precedents in past history one of which was the use of the potato in Ireland.

Figure 6 Table of Approximate Time Humanity Spent
in **each Period** of Farming
(Time Frame in Thousands of years)

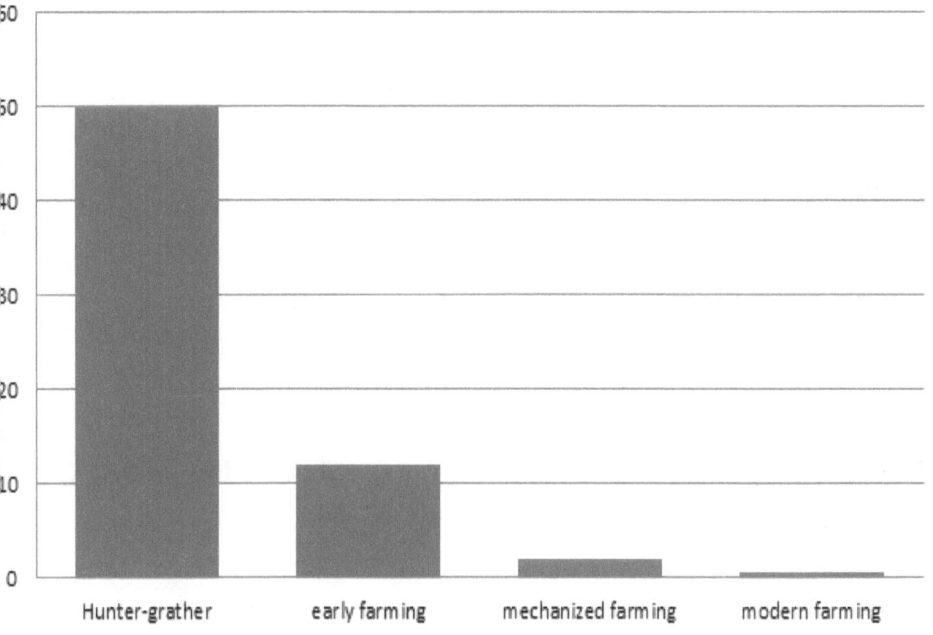

Hunter-gathering-Dominant pre younger dryas human activity
in food production

Early farming- post younger dryas activity in food production
including use of domesticated animals

Mechanized farming-Industrial revolution to 1950s with use of
machines

Modern farming-1965 to present with use of plant modification
and   genetics

Table 9 MAPPING OF RATE OF CHANGE OF FARMING TECHNOLOGY IN RESPONSE TO POPULATION SIZE IN BILLIONS

	1800	1945	1965	2010
Population	1	2	3	6.5
Farming Technology change	123	33	10	2.5 —

Based on Data from FAO and Farming data and the following information

1987

The first field tests of genetically engineered crops (tobacco and tomato) are conducted in the United States.

1992

Calgene's Favr Savr tomato, engineered to remain firm for a longer period of time, is approved for commercial production by the US Department of Agriculture.

1992

The FDA declares that genetically engineered foods are "not inherently dangerous" and do not require special regulation.

1994

The European Union's first genetically engineered crop, tobacco, is approved in France.

Food , Energy , and Water

2000
International Biosafety Protocol is approved by 130 countries at the Convention on Biological Diversity in Montréal, Canada. The protocol agrees upon labeling of genetically engineered crops, but still needs to be ratified by 50 nations before it goes into effect.

Sources:

MIT		Tech			Review
"About	Biotech"	from	Access		Excellence
Biotechnology	timeline	from	North	Carolina	Biology	Center
United	States	Food	and	Drug	Administration
Organisation for Economic Co-operation and Development Database of Field Trials
Federal	Register,	May	29,	1992
Regulatory Process for Transgeneic Crops in the US from Colorado State University

The introduction of the potato in Ireland occurred within recent history. Irish populations adopted the use of the potato as a food source. However the adoption was not based upon need only, but also upon the desires of the native population. In Ireland a particular type of potato was selected because of its characteristics, which were more desirable for export, and for native consumption. Although there was a wide range in the variety and potatoes available to the Irish, they narrowed their farming efforts to a single species. It was high-yield, but was also susceptible to a particular type of fungus. The potato growth in Ireland proceeded very rapidly and yielded very good results until the selected species was attacked by a fungus. The result was the potato famine. There were other factors contributing to the potato famine, such as the export of large quantities of potatoes while domestic production output was down because of the fungus. In North America where the potato was a native this fungus was not unknown, but because indigenous populations used a wide variety of potential species, the fungus had negligible impact. As the people of Ireland selected a single potato species as their primary production medium, the fungus had a more disastrous impact. This is the problem that we face as human society narrows the number species that it relies upon for food production to a small number of species. As we saw in table 9, the rate of change in food production technology has been reduced significantly over the last 200 years. The interval between changes has decreased rapidly from thousands of years, to a period of time of decades between modifications and alterations in this system. These modifications and alterations usually take the form of new plant species being introduced to accommodate a specific need for population, new fertilization methods to accommodate greater plant yield, or new forming technologies to bring more land into production.

This process of bringing additional land into production has seen unexpected consequences for human populations. Bringing new land sources into production would seem to be a natural process for ensuring continued growth in food production, but that is not necessarily the case. Remember, food production is no longer determined by human needs alone, but also by human desires. Market forces drives production in modern society. Today farmers from Britain purchase large tracts of arable land in the remnants of the Soviet republic to grow food stocks for the tables in Europe. These products seldom make it to the tables of the countries in which they are grown, and are being marketed and developed based upon market forces in Europe. We saw a similar situation just recently as American farmers began to move away from corn production to be sold as government surplus and then resold to other countries as grains because of higher prices in ethanol. Farmers found a potentially lucrative market in ethanol production that would generate many times the revenue for a bushel of corn than selling the same bushel to the government for surplus. These market forces at first seem benign until we realize that other nations were now dependent upon the corn for food stocks and would no longer have it available. The market forces had shifted a large segment of global production and needs for food consumption, to human needs for fuel consumption. The drive of market forces and the shortened interval for rapid change in the food production system makes it possible to shift very rapidly entire sectors of the system to new product lines. This is not an unusual phenomenon, and can be seen in many areas of technology, most notably in Moore's Law as it relates to semiconductor technology.

Moore's law is named after the president of Intel Corporation, who first brought this observation to public attention in a 1965 paper. Although later research has revealed that the principles for this law were identified by several other sources earlier, the observed phenomenon is still most widely known as Moore's Law. This was the first time that it was brought to public attention that computer technology in terms of the density of components on a chip, the number of connections would have to be doubled every 24 months to accommodate human technology. This principal is a self-fulfilling prophecy. As the law became accepted, chip manufacturers used it to project manufacturing schedules which accommodated the principal, and thus fulfilled the principal law. Computer technology doubles chip densities and processing speed every 18 to 24 months. Likewise the same principle can now be inferred in the system of food production. As populations have increased beyond the point of 1 billion the system of food production has been making adjustments more and more rapidly to accommodate growing societal demands. By the time we reach what was commonly known as the Green Revolution, food production systems are increasing the rate of modification to accommodate market forces in the food producing systems. These rapid changes often result in rapid market shifts in food production based upon the desires of technologically advanced civilizations, often at expense of less developed civilizations. Food production is being altered it unseen and unpredictable ways.

Today's world food production system not only determines a society's efficiency, but also its status in the larger world. The United States and Europe, with more sophisticated food producing systems set the standard that much of the rest of the world follows. This has resulted in a greater narrowing of the number of selected species, which are adopted through genetic manipulation, and chemical augmentation to meet growing market demand. There's been much recent discussion about the use of grain products to feed domesticated animals for human consumption. Although this is an inefficient method of moving protein to market, since for every pound of animal flesh it takes several pounds of grain to produce , one would wonder why it is such a prevalent factor in developing countries, where meat production is now becoming a market driving force. This may be largely due to the desire of those developing countries, as they become more economically stable, and the standard of living to approaches that of United States, to show the baby to have the ability, and the wealth to enjoy the status of the American and European people. The result has been an even greater distortion of food producing systems. As we structure these systems to accommodate the growing status of developed and developing countries, we are often ignoring the basic needs of under developed countries.

The most common example of this would be the country of Mexico, the southern neighbor to the United States. Recent New York Times articles have revealed the story of how Mexican farmers or required to buy Genetic seeds from the United States border to continue production of the primary crop in Mexico, which is corn. Genetically engineered seed stocks are expensive, and Mexican farmers have little money with which to buy them. However Mexico represents $40 billion to the American agribusiness interests in the United States and the developed world. To countries such as United States with a gross domestic product in the trillions of dollars, this might seem to be a small amount for country to pay for stabled Agriculture. For Mexico it is an amount which is excessive, and which leaves many Mexican farmers unable to continue in the business of farming.

Food , Energy , and Water

The question which remains is whether this pillar, this system, necessary for human survival can withstand the test of time, or will it succumb to outside forces because of its sophisticated, yet fragile nature. The remaining principal to be analyzed is how sophisticated systems respond to outside forces, or attacks. The more sophisticated and complex system, the more susceptible it is true and attacked, and this becomes especially true for a system of food production which is focused on a complex, yet very narrow group of species. Most recently we have had examples of what happens when a single species is removed for a short period of time. The result can often be catastrophic. As social pressures, and market pressures increasingly moves this system to specialization in these limited species will it be able to sustain itself and remained stable if there is a significant outside shock to the system. Comparable examples to view might be what happened to the large and very complex structures created by North American natives, which ultimately collapsed as a result of contact with European forces. (There's a growing body of evidence that American groups in South, Central and North America had developed sophisticated societies and farming technologies, they did not survive the first significant shock from outside forces.) Will the system that we have in place today follow that same example as it comes in contact with new forces, or is it more robust. Currently scientists are evaluating what they termed planetary principles which may have a significant impact not only on this systems but on the globe, and our species and its survival. Will the system we have in place maintain us or zero ultimately fail us. Only time will tell.

Yet food production is only one third of the critical systems necessary for human survival. The other two systems are just as complex, sophisticated, and fragile and are intertwined with the production of food as systems necessary for human survival.

Energy: The new Vital System of Technology

The study of energy is the study of the systems of technology that utilize it, and is a study in inequality. One need only look at Table 10 and Table 11 to see how energy consumption and population bear a striking resemblance to each other. Table 10 gives a look at energy consumption in all countries per person for three selected years. The difference between developed and developing countries is pronounced. In table 11 we see how individual regions show the same large disparity.

Table 10 Energy Consumption: Total energy consumption per   capita
Units: Kilograms of oil equivalent (kgoe) per person by selected year

country	1990	2000	2005
Albania	809.0	594.0	767.0
Algeria	943.0	960.0	1,058.0
Angola	597.0	572.0	621.0
Argentina	1,415.0	1,679.0	1,644.0
Armenia	2,240.0	672.0	848.0
Australia	5,106.3	5,737.0	5,897.5
Austria	3,263.1	3,624.5	4,134.7
Azerbaijan	3,637.0	1,430.0	1,649.0
Bahrain	9,796.0	9,278.0	11,180.0

Food , Energy , and Water

Bangladesh	123.0	145.0	171.0
Belarus	4,139.0	2,459.0	2,720.0
Belgium	4,988.0	6,040.7	5,891.7
Benin	324.0	279.0	306.0
Bolivia	416.0	594.0	578.0
Bosnia and Herzegovina	1,633.0	1,044.0	1,270.0
Botswana	890.0	1,050.0	1,073.0
Brazil	897.0	1,068.0	1,124.0
Brunei Darussalam	7,070.0	7,633.0	7,062.0
Bulgaria	3,306.0	2,322.0	2,592.0
Cambodia	0.0	321.0	354.0
Cameroon	432.0	428.0	428.0
Canada	7,564.0	8,214.5	8,472.6
Côte d'Ivoire	348.0	410.0	432.0
Chile	1,067.0	1,684.0	1,815.0
China	760.0	875.0	1,316.0
Colombia	708.0	651.0	627.0
Congo	425.0	247.0	300.0
Congo, Dem Rep	315.0	295.0	295.0
Costa Rica	658.0	842.0	883.0
Croatia	1,897.0	1,726.0	2,000.0
Cuba	1,597.0	1,034.0	905.0
Cyprus	2,791.0	3,499.0	3,367.0
Czech Rep	4,726.0	3,934.0	4,418.6

Denmark	3,485.8	3,627.6	3,634.3
Dominican Rep	584.0	944.0	827.0
Ecuador	597.0	674.0	789.0
Egypt	573.0	676.0	828.0
El Salvador	496.0	649.0	673.0
Eritrea	0.0	203.0	175.0
Estonia	6,107.0	3,306.0	3,786.0
Ethiopia	296.0	291.0	304.0
Finland	5,758.0	6,270.0	6,555.0
France	3,912.6	4,250.3	4,396.8
Gabon	1,299.0	1,212.0	1,243.0
Georgia	2,259.0	613.0	718.0
Germany	4,481.2	4,175.3	4,187.0
Ghana	345.0	397.0	404.0
Gibraltar	2,294.0	4,775.0	5,432.0
Greece	2,150.6	2,555.7	2,794.0
Guatemala	504.0	640.0	634.0
Haiti	231.0	257.0	293.0
Honduras	496.0	469.0	537.0
Hong Kong	1,869.0	2,385.0	2,603.0
Hungary	2,755.4	2,449.8	2,757.4
Iceland	8,476.1	11,502.7	12,209.4
India	377.0	452.0	491.0
Indonesia	579.0	740.0	814.0

Food , Energy , and Water

Iran, Islamic Rep	1,264.0	1,864.0	2,381.0
Iraq	1,029.0	1,037.0	1,067.0
Ireland	2,942.6	3,732.0	3,656.0
Israel	2,599.0	3,057.0	2,816.0
Italy	2,610.6	3,043.2	3,169.1
Jamaica	1,232.0	1,514.0	1,445.0
Japan	3,595.1	4,151.8	4,135.3
Jordan	1,103.0	1,068.0	1,296.0
Kazakhstan	4,505.0	2,596.0	3,462.0
Kenya	533.0	490.0	503.0
Korea, Dem People's Rep	1,670.0	903.0	943.0
Korea, Rep	2,178.0	4,029.6	4,415.4
Kuwait	3,985.0	9,320.0	11,102.0
Kyrgyzstan	1,723.0	498.0	544.0
Latvia	2,915.0	1,644.0	2,050.0
Lebanon	843.0	1,489.0	1,559.0
Libyan Arab Jamahiriya	2,663.0	3,208.0	3,254.0
Lithuania	4,377.0	2,034.0	2,515.0
Luxembourg	9,277.6	8,284.5	10,137.8
Macedonia, FYR	1,421.0	1,348.0	1,346.0
Malaysia	1,307.0	2,229.0	2,418.0
Malta	2,151.0	2,012.0	2,349.0
Mexico	1,514.0	1,528.2	1,701.2
Moldova, Rep	2,290.0	671.0	845.0

Mongolia	1,525.0	895.0	916.0
Morocco	281.0	358.0	458.0
Mozambique	536.0	484.0	516.0
Myanmar	262.0	263.0	291.0
Namibia	0.0	544.0	679.0
Nepal	304.0	334.0	338.0
Netherlands	4,490.6	4,798.7	5,048.8
Netherlands Antilles	7,819.0	7,893.0	9,057.0
New Zealand	4,093.5	4,687.2	4,218.0
Nicaragua	535.0	559.0	648.0
Nigeria	783.0	759.0	789.0
Norway	5,050.7	5,723.8	7,153.2
Oman	2,476.0	3,960.0	5,440.0
Pakistan	402.0	463.0	490.0
Panama	618.0	875.0	804.0
Paraguay	731.0	723.0	673.0
Peru	458.0	483.0	494.0
Philippines	428.0	560.0	538.0
Poland	2,626.1	2,336.7	2,429.0
Portugal	1,725.0	2,468.4	2,574.1
Qatar	13,554.0	19,585.0	19,466.0
Romania	2,689.0	1,616.0	1,772.0
Russian Federation	5,923.0	4,196.0	4,519.0
Saudi Arabia	3,744.0	5,169.0	6,068.0

Food , Energy , and Water

Senegal	281.0	256.0	261.0
Serbia and Montenegro	1,851.0	1,640.0	2,066.0
Singapore	4,384.0	5,537.0	6,932.0
Slovakia	4,023.2	3,290.1	3,502.8
Slovenia	2,801.0	3,260.0	3,655.0
South Africa	2,592.0	2,525.0	2,722.0
Spain	2,337.8	3,096.0	3,339.6
Sri Lanka	324.0	418.0	478.0
Sudan	408.0	419.0	508.0
Sweden	5,556.8	5,439.3	5,780.3
Switzerland	3,649.8	3,606.3	3,599.3
Syrian Arab Rep	909.0	1,045.0	940.0
Taiwan	2,372.0	3,749.0	4,621.0
Tajikistan	1,055.0	464.0	531.0
Tanzania	374.0	387.0	532.0
Thailand	803.0	1,214.0	1,557.0
Togo	365.0	329.0	325.0
Trinidad and Tobago	4,969.0	7,670.0	9,736.0
Tunisia	679.0	794.0	843.0
Turkey	941.9	1,139.5	1,185.9
Turkmenistan	5,353.0	3,215.0	3,381.0
Ukraine	4,851.0	2,727.0	3,043.0
United Arab Emirates	12,716.0	11,023.0	10,354.0
United Kingdom	3,708.8	3,971.4	3,894.6

United States	7,699.5	8,151.8	7,885.9
Uruguay	725.0	921.0	836.0
Uzbekistan	2,262.0	2,044.0	1,798.0
Venezuela	2,224.0	2,333.0	2,293.0
Viet Nam	367.0	477.0	617.0
Yemen	212.0	272.0	321.0
Zambia	653.0	586.0	611.0
Zimbabwe	888.0	796.0	747.0

Food , Energy , and Water

Information   collected   from   DOE   and   EIA   data   in   2003

World Primary Energy Consumption (Btu), 1992-2000 (Quadrillion (10^{15}) Btu)									
Region	1992	1993	1994	1995	1996	1997	1998	1999	2000
North America Total	102.14	104.38	106.63	108.57	112.20	113.01	113.34	115.79	118.67
Central & South America Total	15.33	16.11	16.77	17.54	18.50	19.38	20.11	20.36	20.99
Western Europe Total	64.24	64.65	64.71	66.71	68.46	68.94	70.30	70.36	71.54
Eastern Europe & Former U.S.S.R Total	65.16	60.75	54.68	53.25	52.47	49.82	48.81	49.49	50.48
Middle East Total	12.03	12.73	13.37	13.93	14.61	15.44	16.19	16.61	17.28
Afric Total	9.92	9.96	10.43	10.64	10.91	11.40	11.30	11.61	11.95
Asia & Oceania Total	81.60	86.71	92.25	97.61	100.77	104.05	103.04	105.36	107.98
World Total	350.43	355.28	358.84	368.25	377.93	382.04	383.09	389.58	398.88

Table 11 Energy Consumption by Region

Energy is the lifeblood without which modern societies cannot function, or survive.   In today's world developed countries consume large quantities of energy to keep their technologies running and their societies happy. Yet, population pressures are making the competition for energy more volatile. In order to keep modern technology is running smoothly, a country must have a continuous and uninterrupted supply of energy. Developing countries, as they struggle to move from developing status into a developed status seek ever growing supplies of energy for their growing societies. This competition

115

is not based on fairness, or a level playing field. It is based upon a survival of the fittest mentality which pits the majority of the population against a minority of the population which controls the technology and with it the ability to produce energy most effectively.

As seen in the study of agricultural technology and food producing systems, perception shaped the reality of societies. Reality has little to do with these perceptions that shape our modern society. Countries with a large technological base use huge amounts of energy and are deemed a success. Although we have grown concerned over the last several decades about the impact of technology, there is no argument to be made about technology and success as being hand-in-hand. Developing societies in the modern world use technology and become trapped in a vicious circle of pursuing energy to maintain technology, and developing technology to pursue energy. This vicious circle often shapes our perceptions and what we perceived as reality. The book written by Richard Wilkinson, "*The impact of inequality: How to make sick societies healthier*", is an interesting study in how perceptions and the necessity to maintain inequality shapes our modern world. Too often anxieties and insecurities drive modern society rather than rational and reasoned thought. We often cannot see what to change, or recognize what needs to be changed, because we are blind to the psychological forces, or psycho social forces that have an increasingly important impact in our world. A country is less likely to give up its place of advantage, obtained by technology, and will be willing to do whatever is necessary to maintain the status quo even when that means keeping billions of other people in relative poverty. It is often only when shame, becomes the dominant emotion that advanced societies begin the process of dialogue, and accommodation, with their more numerous partners in the world. We see this in cases such as Darfur, or the continuing food crises of Africa. Technology and its need for energy take us in a spiral of activity which escalates and becomes more frantic with each succeeding generation of technology. In today's world technology grows at an ever-increasing rate based upon Moore's law as explained earlier. We have moved from the steam engine, through the era of the internal combustion engine, to the era of the Internet. With each of these changes, developed societies have moved to different levels of consumption, and different types of energy necessary to run their societies. It may be useful at this time to take full look at the history of energy consumption in the modern technological society from its modest beginnings in the industrial revolution.

ARTHUR JACKSON

Energy and the Industrial Revolution

The industrial revolution was a turning point in human evolution. Population growth increased steadily to reach a critical mass at 1 billion people. The local village had become the modern urban center. The local farmer had given way to industrial manufacturing, which became the center of human endeavors. These new urban complexes would mark a change in energy needs to fuel the manufacturing facilities that would be borne out of a complex of human interactions. As more and more people moved into cities, three prime ingredients came together to fuel this change. There was an abundance of human labor, cheap local energy , and the new level of technology called mechanization. This new technological process would consume ever-increasing amounts of energy, and would soon replace animal power from domestication as the chief source of human technology.

As large groups of people moved into industrial centers, human populations were approaching a critical nexus. . In many species population density can reach a critical point where the behavior of the species is radically changed. Scientists recently began to document this behavior in such insect species as grasshoppers, or locust. With numbers below the threshold level their activities are benign when compared to what happens as their populations increase in response to a large food supply. As populations grow in response to food supply the locusts reach a critical point and began to exhibit behavior which is radically different. They go from reluctant and somewhat shy creatures that avoid gathering in large groups into an almost new species that actively seeks group participation and they begin to function as a group. This is the result of chemical changes that occur in response to population density pressures. This change in behavior has been seen to result in a swarm mode that sets them on a path of destruction, which often devastates crops in large regions. It is only recently that science has been able to document these chemical changes as a result of increased population pressure in species. Was it similar pressure which began to push human endeavors away from activities of a hunter gatherers species to modern society? When human population was below the threshold level of 1 billion members, some degree of large-scale hunter-gatherer's activity was still available. But, as human populations crossed the threshold of 1 billion they have forever left the ability to engage in any type of large scale hunter gathering activities. Humans will never be able to return to that type of activity as their numbers remain so large. In time isolated city-state's would be transformed it into human

Metroplexes, with continuous ongoing contact with each other and the establishment of exchanges in technology, culture, and commerce between the complexes. The new focus would be on decentralized activities of a group nature, which cause a resultant change in technology and energy consumption to accommodate.

The pre industrial human society had minimal energy needs. As we can see from Table 12 the per-capita requirement for energy escalated many fold between hunter-gatherer and modern man.

Daily Consumption of Energy Per Capita

	Technological Man	Industrial Man	Advanced Agricultural Man	Primitive Agricultural Man	Hunting Man	Primitive Man
☐ Transportation	63	14	1			
☐ Industry and Agriculture	91	24	7	4		
■ Home and Commerce	66	32	12	4	2	
▣ Food	10	7	6	4	3	2

Table 12 Estimated Daily Consumption of Energy per Capita at Different Historical Points Adapted from: E. Cook, "The Flow of Energy in an Industrial Society" Scientific American, 1971 p. 135.

It would not be long before society began to look for a common fuel source to meet the growing needs of industrialization. In Europe, with its complex of Independent States, they moved rapidly into a posture of trade and negotiations for resources, fuel, and manufactured products, to become the first society to move successfully away from animal labor, and human labor to industrialized systems. In England large scale manufacturing was well under way. This required the creation of a large rail system that could be used to transport completed product, people, foodstuffs, and fuel to maintain the industrial complex and to keep it operating. As the system expanded, it would require additional energy.

Undoubtedly, the expansion of the systems would create an imbalance that would in time come to be known as the division of labor. It would create a structure of haves and have-nots. Those who dominated and controlled the instrumentation of technology, where the haves. Those that work to fuel supply and maintain the systems were the have-nots. Modern industrialization was establishing a new system of inequality. Energy would become one of the key components traded with-in this system. Countries, and individuals would trade energy in one form or another, depending upon the amount of surplus that they as individuals possessed.

Food , Energy , and Water

Humanity would apply the principles of Mundell's unholy trinity in the system of energy production. In the early stages of industrialization, coal was a primary energy source, which quickly displaced whale oil, and other energy sources because of its abundance, and its BTU output per unit. The use of new technology made the removal, extraction, transportation, and utilization of this energy source relatively easy for those nations that had access to industrialized technology. Instead of using human or animal power, which would require that a significant portion of the energy you produced be used to maintain the additional labor force, companies could use large steam driven machines that would operate twenty four hours a day. These machines would take the place of hundreds of workers and gradually reduce costs for the production of energy. Coal quickly became a highly sought after commodity. Many nations in Europe had access to large coal deposits with-in the borders of their respective countries. Despite this fact, coal would have to be transported across different regions of individual countries as industrial centers sprang up throughout nations. Ultimately, countries would begin to trade with each other as sources of coal from one country might be more accessible to a competitor that its own coal sources. This would create the need for countries to establish either an independent energy system which would mean isolation from its competitors, or a system with mobility and a stable exchange rate with competing countries. You could have two, but not all three of these factors as Robert Mundell had established in his unholy trinity. As countries chose mobile energy, with a stable exchange rate, this basic principle would spur commerce between countries in Europe and promote technological change and foster the establishment of a monolithic energy policy in much of Europe. Rather than striking out to develop a different energy system, it would be much easier for countries to exchange energy with each other if there was a common source for all countries. In this regard the system, and the resultant rule helped to generate a unified policy on energy.

Even in the Americas, where industrialization was just beginning to take hold, we would see the establishment of a uniform policy of energy production in the eastern portion of the United States where industrialization was to start first. First, companies, then states would develop sources of coal as they worked to rapidly keep pace with the industrialized efforts of Europe. Coal-fired systems would dominate until well into the 19th century. It was the primary source of energy for the new mechanized steam engines that were quickly changing the industrial landscape of Europe and America. With each expansion of industrial facilities new energy requirements would need to be put into place to accommodate the transfer of finished product, and the exchange of energy sources for fuel. Transportation systems would become very important in the expansion of Modern industrialization.

From the 17th through the 18th century there would be a frantic effort to establish new rail systems throughout most industrialized nations. These land base systems were essential to transport completed product to different portions of the country, and to transport much needed energy to the industrial complexes to keep them in operation. It was not long before railroads would become a transportation system for people, as well as product. The Metroplexes of Europe and the United States were becoming connected through a growing system of railroads. In Europe during this time, there was a great deal of railroad building occurring within each of the industrialized nations as indicated in table 13.

ARTHUR JACKSON

Table 13 spread of Railways in Ten Selected Countries

(Length of line open [in kilometers [1km = 5/8 mile])

	1840	1860	1880	1900
Austria-Hungary	144	4,543	18,507	36,330
Belgium	334	1,730	4,112	4,591
France	496	9,167	23,089	38,109
Germany	469	11,089	33,838	51,678
Great Britain	2,390	14,603	25,060	30,079
Italy	20	2,404	9,290	16,429
Netherlands	17	335	1,846	2,776
Russia	27	1,626	22,865	53,234
Spain	-	1,917	7,490	13,214
Sweden	-	527	5,876	11,303

Reprinted from the Modern History Source Book, 2005

The Rise of The Urban center

The study of the rise of urban centers, is really a study in the energy utilization. The industrial revolution created a new relationship between population density and social development. In the early stages of the industrial revolution urban complexes were refuges for peasants, displaced farmers, and other down on their luck social groups. As social forces began to organize themselves into strong central governments, rural populations were displaced from the countryside. The new cities, with their new technologies, offered a meeting of three critical components for the industrial revolution. Displaced populations were cheap labor, a critical ingredient to making industrialization economically feasible. The availability of a ready source of energy, and the energy source being relatively uniform across many countries were the necessary ingredients to make the industrial revolution take hold. Industrialization evolving out of England, would not have been easy to copy for countries such as France, Germany, Russia, or eventually the Americas, without the existence of a common fuel source, in this case coal. The existence of this fuel source made the emerging technologies easily transportable, or mobile, and would establish uniform exchange between countries as common technologies based upon a common fuel source would begin to take hold. In these early days of urbanization, population size began to grow. But, it is not population size which is the driving factor for human development, but population density. As we can see in table 14, population size throughout Europe from the early 500 BP to 1450 BP. Growth was slow and was stable, but did not create the pressures of population density to be exhibited in the industrial revolution. This new paradigm of very dense populations would have a dramatic effect on both human biological behavior, economic behavior, and social behavior.

Table 14 Population Estimates (in millions) at specified times 500-1340

AREA	500	650	1000	1340
Greece/Balkans	5	3	5	6
Italy	4	2.5	5	10
Spain/Portugal	4	3.5	7	9
Total - South	13	9	17	25
France/Low countries	5	3	6	19
British Isles	0.5	0.5	2	5
Germany/Scandinavia	3.5	2	4	11.5
Total - West/Central	9	5.5	12	35.5
Slavia.	5	3		
---Russia			6	8
---Poland/Lithuania			2	3
Hungary	0.5	0.5	1.5	2
Total -East	5.5	3.5	9.5	13
TOTAL EUROPE	27.5	18	38.5	73.5

The information here is taken from Josiah C. Russell, "Population in Europe:, in Carlo M. Cipolla, ed., *The Fontana Economic History of Europe*, Vol. I: The Middle Ages, (Glasgow : Collins/Fontana, 1972), 25-71 This text is part of the Internet Medieval Source Book. The Sourcebook is a collection of public domain and copy-permitted texts related to medieval and Byzantine history.

Urban centers began development largely around the new model of manufacturing. Manufacturing centers as business models became places to employ large numbers of people at relatively cheap wages. It also marked a shift from the basic model of food production as the primary commodity, to one in which energy became the primary source of evaluating development. As was shown previously, the hunter gatherer used very little energy for anything other than food collection. The human beings in the industrial revolution would use increasing amounts of energy in ever more diverse ways. The first example of this is the change in biological behavior that the modern urban complex would have on humanity. As manufacturing and business interest began to take hold and dominate the social framework, the need to move a larger and larger number of people into small compressed areas became vital. A long with the changes in population density, human behavior would be modified in ways that would promote and stabilize human productivity. Population densities would become the driving force for divergence away from purely economic models, to true social reform, as societies began to invest larger and larger numbers of their populations in urban centers. The need to control social behavior, the creation of centers of artistic development, education, entertainment all evolved out of population density pressures in the urban complex. Along with each change in population density was a requirement for additional energy. Suddenly a worker in industrialized Europe would find themselves competing with other workers for additional sources of energy. The more energy one had available, the more successful the individual would be. The great driving force as population densities continue to increase is the accumulation of energy in various forms. You are successful if you had not just basic foodstuffs, but had a certain quota of meat available to the family throughout the week. This resulting pressure within the urban complex changed the way farmers would select specific crops for market. The move toward a more prominent meat based society focused farming efforts toward directing more energy into the production of livestock, to meet the rising social requirements. There was also a growing need to provide not just basic shelter, but shelter which denoted ones changing status with in society. Houses became not simple rooms, but multi room dwellings with the resultant requirements for additional heat, light, and energy input to construct. It would also change the very social structure of human society.

The need to entertain growing numbers of people would require the creation of social organizations to provide entertainment, and ultimately give rise to the arts. We would

131

also see the eventual creation of education systems. Children were not simply a source of labor, but were the future of societies, and as such required preparation and indoctrination to become productive citizens with in society. This would require the building of school, administration facilities and transportation systems with the resultant additional amount of energy as education became an important, if not primary factor for many evolving urban centers. I make note of the comparison between Europe and United States as some of the earliest institutions of learning were set up by churches. City and state governments would eventually take over the role of education as formal school systems were established and became mandatory in the late 18th hundreds.

Each of the biological changes and social changes also carried with them an impact on the amount of energy each person would require for their day-to-day living. The urban complexes would become the driving forces to shape not only themselves, but the entire regions around them. Human behavior would be forever modified and adopted to these new conditions. Today modern cities are only able to exist because of the social systems created by growing population density in the earlier urban centers.

As discussed before these biological and social changes would also engender economic changes. As strong central governments came into existence, and took over the operation of urban centers, there would be a growing need to provide economic incentives and stability for the growing populations. Governments would be required to expend energy ,money and effort to, not only control and regulate economic enterprise, but to monitor that enterprise for tax purposes.

As you begin to see urban complexes expanded role throughout the latter 17th and 18th centuries, we also see with them the expansion of central governments. With this expansion came an increasing variety of rules and regulations controlling human behavior and business behavior. Regulation required energy to implement and enforce laws that would vary by region. Cities would create their own rules necessary to monitor their populations, which would be subordinate to counties or other next level entities, which would be subordinate to states or regions, and finally to a strong federal government. With each of these changes the amount of energy required will increase exponentially. Social changes would also mandate the way in which communication, technological advancements, and transportation would develop within the urban center. The extension of transportation services between the centers establishment of communication and an exchange of technology, in the urban complex itself, along with growing population density would demand an increasing network of energy dependent systems to facilitate continued urban expansion. The need to be able to determine the number people within a given structure would become critical in certain instances such as emergencies, fires, or other disasters.

It would become more and more important that individuals be able to maneuver across the urban complex as jobs moved, and people had to move with the jobs. This would create a growing network of roads throughout the urban center to facilitate movement, and also a growing network of communication to facilitate transmission of information. The modern high-rise city would not be possible without the creation of the elevator, or climate control. A vital function since as urban centers grow they tend to create huge heat sinks which must be dealt with if the populations are to survive. The modern high rise would not be livable without these systems. Yet each requires increasing levels of energy to operate and maintain.

As we move from our rural past to the more urbanized future we will see a dramatic shift in the percentage of population living in urban centers. It is expected that within the next few years more than 80% of all human society will reside in urban Metroplexes. We will see the population in Asia rise from 1. 6 billion people living in urban centers to more than 2.7

billion people. Countries such as Africa will increase their urban representation from approximately 250 million people to almost one billion people by 2027. A great deal of this growth will occur in populations are growing faster than developing countries. The result will be that more than 80% been of all human society will reside in an urban center within the next 75 years. These growing urban complexes will change the very structure of the world. Looking at the development of some of the centers in Asia, particularly in China we can see the impact these new centers of highly dense humans will have upon the earth's geography. When a recent study was conducted in one of the busiest port regions in China and a number of other cities in the region by researchers who compiled readings from 16 meteorological stations in the region and compared them to maps derived from NASA, to chart urban growth and its impact something new was seen. The study was published in The Journal of climate covered the time frame between 1988 and 1996. The study found that the growing urban centers were having a pronounced impact on weather patterns in the region. This team created a statistical model which linked urban growth and rain fall and found that they impacted negatively on overall moisture production. Large metroplexes, with their huge consumption of energy cause an umbrella effect as result of the amount of heat generated by the structures in close concentration. As more and more urban complexes come into existence, we will begin to see an even greater demand for energy to accommodate these needs, and perhaps, a more pronounced impact on rainfall, and ultimately weather.

China uses coal, the dominant source of fuel used by industrialized nations until the early 19th century, as it's dominate energy source. Just as in the industrialized nations of the past, it was the need for greater energy sources that has prompted the development of hydrocarbons as a fuel source in China. Hydrocarbons are not new, and have been available since the early 14th century. In parts of the Middle East tribes would often use the material oozing out of ground as a fuel source. It would take the development of the internal combustion engine, to make this source the new replacement for coal. Hydrocarbons are not just a high energy source. They can be distilled into a growing number of products for commercial use. Like coal, hydrocarbons also made it possible, and relatively easy to adopt as a uniform system of energy in the form of gasoline, or diesel fuel that made large urban societies mobile. Humanity was now not linked simply by railroads, but by network of highways. By the end of World War Two, major road building enterprises had begun in most of the industrialized world, and were soon followed by similar booms in the developing countries. With populations mobility came an additional increase in energy demand. It was now possible for individuals to reside many miles away from the area in which they might work. This new transportation demand would create a great need for this new energy source.

The first modern oil well was drilled in Asia, in the first half of the 18th century. The distillation of by products was first undertaken in 1849 by a Canadian geologist by the name of Dr. Abraham Gesner. Dr. Gesner was looking for a replacement for whale oil, and developed the distillate kerosene. It would be in the 1850's when the first commercial well was drilled in Poland, but it would be North America that would truly launch a hydrocarbon revolution in Pennsylvania. From oil wells in the 1890's to modern offshore platforms in the Gulf and deep waters of the oceans, hydrocarbon has become the primary fuel source for modern technology.

Today, energy expended in the search of energy, is as intensive as the consumption of the product itself. Drilling is a global enterprise that pits developed countries against developing countries. A country cannot hope to compete successfully in the global arena without access to a continuous and uninterrupted supply of oil. Today the center of oil technology is in the Middle East, which currently has the largest establish resources. Yet, global exploration continues to expand the range and depth of exploration activities for this precious commodity. It is currently the lifeblood of society and technology. This energy source does not just provide the gasoline to make society mobile, it provides plastics, chemicals, drugs, and fertilizers to make the green revolution possible. The need for energy continues to grow as human societies continue to trade in ever increasing quantities of the precious commodity.

No single energy source can meet all human needs. In an effort to balance the need for energy we have begun to diversify the energy sources that we use. As shown in Table 15 coal is once again emerging as a primary source of energy in world. But diversification of energy resources is the requirement of the day. Coal, natural gas, oil, nuclear, and hydroelectric as well as other sources of power are all being tapped to meet the growing energy demand of human society.

Food , Energy , and Water

Table 15 World Primary Energy Production by Source, 1970-2005
Source; EIA International data base 1970 forward
(Quadrillion Btu)

Year	Coal	Natural Gas [1]	Crude Oil [2]	Natural Gas Plant Liquids	Nuclear Electric Power [3]	Hydroelectric Power [3]	Geothermal [3] and Other [4]	Total
1970	62.96	37.09	97.09	3.61	0.90	12.15	1.59	215.39
1971	61.72	39.80	102.70	3.85	1.23	12.74	1.61	223.64
1972	63.65	42.08	108.52	4.09	1.66	13.31	1.68	234.99
1973	63.87	44.44	117.88	4.23	2.15	13.52	1.73	247.83
1974	63.79	45.35	117.82	4.22	2.86	14.84	1.76	250.64
1975	66.20	45.67	113.08	4.12	3.85	15.03	1.74	249.69
1976	67.32	47.62	122.92	4.24	4.52	15.08	1.97	263.67
1977	68.46	48.85	127.75	4.40	5.41	15.56	2.11	272.54
1978	69.56	50.26	128.51	4.55	6.42	16.80	2.32	278.41
1979	73.83	53.93	133.87	4.87	6.69	17.69	2.48	293.36
1980	[R]71.27	54.73	128.04	5.10	7.58	17.90	2.94	[R]287.56
1981	[R]71.68	55.56	120.11	5.37	8.53	18.26	3.10	[R]282.61
1982	[R]74.33	55.49	114.45	5.35	9.51	18.71	[R]3.28	281.13
1983	[R]74.33	56.12	[R]113.98	5.36	10.72	19.69	[R]3.58	283.78
1984	[R]78.46	61.78	116.88	5.73	12.99	20.19	3.73	[R]299.76
1985	[R]82.28	64.22	115.37	5.83	15.30	20.42	3.82	[R]307.24
1986	[R]84.32	65.32	120.18	6.15	16.25	20.89	[R]3.82	[R]316.93
1987	[R]86.10	68.48	[R]121.08	6.35	17.64	20.90	[R]3.84	324.39
1988	[R]87.98	71.80	125.84	6.65	19.23	21.48	[R]4.01	[R]336.99
1989	[R]89.58	74.24	127.83	6.69	19.74	21.53	[R]4.38	[R]344.00
1990	91.02	[R]76.06	129.35	6.87	20.36	22.35	3.98	[R]349.99
1991	[R]86.41	[R]76.88	128.73	7.12	21.18	22.83	4.08	[R]347.23
1992	[R]86.23	[R]77.08	128.93	7.17	21.28	22.71	[R]4.34	347.74
1993	[R]84.41	[R]78.59	128.72	7.47	22.01	23.94	[R]4.37	[R]349.51
1994	86.46	[R]79.35	130.69	8.10	22.41	24.15	[R]4.56	[R]355.72
1995	[R]88.55	[R]80.42	133.43	8.40	23.26	25.34	[R]4.71	[R]364.11
1996	[R]89.15	[R]84.16	136.73	8.59	24.11	25.79	[R]4.86	[R]373.40
1997	[R]92.87	[R]84.11	140.63	8.79	23.88	26.07	[R]4.97	381.32

139

1998	[R]91.53	[R]85.75	143.24	9.02	24.32	26.05	[R]4.96	[R]384.87
1999	[R]91.12	[R]87.66	140.95	9.26	25.09	26.55	[R]5.16	[K]385.79
2000	[R]90.43	[R]90.99	146.83	9.63	[R]25.65	[R]26.78	[R]5.42	[R]395.72
2001	[R]95.70	[R]93.31	145.57	10.10	26.39	[R]26.56	[R]5.19	[K]402.82
2002	[R]97.65	[R]96.32	[R]143.53	10.28	[R]26.67	[R]26.53	[R]5.53	[K]406.50
2003	[R]105.34	[R]98.50	[R]148.41	10.74	[R]26.37	26.79	[R]5.90	[R]422.05
2004	[R]114.10	[R]101.50	[R]155.38	11.10	[R]27.32	[R]27.89	[R]6.41	[R]443.69
2005	[K]122.07	[K]104.75	[R]157.65	11.47	[R]27.54	[R]28.98	[R]6.88	[K]459.34

Just as we related to food by exponentially decreasing the amount of time that each new development in agriculture would take place, we see of comparable correlation to Moores law in energy consumption. Human consumption experiences a comparable increase as society has become more and more complex, and more and more dependent on energy as the primary source of exchange. Individual consumption rates have grown dramatically and so have the associated cost. It is probably more accurate to evaluate a person by their energy consumption than dollar wealth in today's world. Today each individual in the industrialized world consumes over 1 million BTU of energy daily. Typical values of energy consumption and associated costs are given in Table 16. BTU stands for British Thermal Unit, a measure of energy. One BTU is equal to 0.25 food calories or about the amount of energy in the tip of a match. To put this in perspective, the food energy in a peanut butter and jelly sandwich is about 1250 BTU, one kilowatt hour of electricity is equivalent to 3,412 BTU, a gallon of gasoline contains about 125,000 BTU, and one short ton of coal (2000 lbs) contains about 20 million BTU.

Table 16   Energy Consumption and Expenditures 1949-2008

Year	Energy Consumption	Energy Consumption per Person	Energy Expenditures [1]	Energy Expenditures [1] per Person	Gross Domestic Product (GDP)	Energy Expenditures [1] as Share of GDP	Gross Domestic Product (GDP)	Energy Consumption per Real Dollar of GDP
	Quadrillion Btu	Million Btu	Million Nominal Dollars [4]	Nominal Dollars [4]	Billion Nominal Dollars [4]	Percent	Billion Chained (2000) Dollars [5]	Thousand Btu per Chained (2000) Dollar [8]
1949	31.98	214	NA	NA	267.3	NA	1,634.6	19.57
1950	34.62	227	NA	NA	293.8	NA	1,777.3	19.48
1951	36.97	239	NA	NA	339.3	NA	1,915.0	19.31
1952	36.75	233	NA	NA	358.3	NA	1,988.3	18.48
1953	37.66	235	NA	NA	379.4	NA	2,079.5	18.11
1954	36.64	225	NA	NA	380.4	NA	2,065.4	17.74
1955	40.21	242	NA	NA	414.8	NA	2,212.8	18.17
1956	41.75	247	NA	NA	437.5	NA	2,255.8	18.51
1957	41.79	243	NA	NA	461.1	NA	2,301.1	18.16
1958	41.65	238	NA	NA	467.2	NA	2,279.2	18.27
1959	43.47	244	NA	NA	506.6	NA	2,441.3	17.80
1960	45.09	250	NA	NA	526.4	NA	2,501.8	18.02
1961	45.74	249	NA	NA	544.7	NA	2,560.0	17.87
1962	47.83	256	NA	NA	585.6	NA	2,715.2	17.61
1963	49.65	262	NA	NA	617.7	NA	2,834.0	17.52
1964	51.82	270	NA	NA	663.6	NA	2,998.6	17.28
1965	54.02	278	NA	NA	719.1	NA	3,191.1	16.93
1966	57.02	290	NA	NA	787.8	NA	3,399.1	16.77
1967	58.91	296	NA	NA	832.6	NA	3,484.6	16.91
1968	62.42	311	NA	NA	910.0	NA	3,652.7	17.09
1969	65.62	324	NA	NA	984.6	NA	3,765.4	17.43
1970	67.84	331	82,911	404	1,038.5	8.0	3,771.9	17.99
1971	69.29	334	90,071	434	1,127.1	8.0	3,898.6	17.77
1972	72.70	346	98,108	467	1,238.3	7.9	4,105.0	17.71
1973	75.71	357	111,928	528	1,382.7	8.1	4,341.5	17.44
1974	73.99	346	153,370	717	1,500.0	10.2	4,319.6	17.13
1975	72.00	333	171,846	796	1,638.3	10.5	4,311.2	16.70
1976	76.01	349	193,897	889	1,825.3	10.6	4,540.9	16.74

1977	78.00	354	220,461	1,001	2,030.9	10.9	4,750.5	16.42
1978	79.99	359	239,230	1,075	2,294.7	10.4	5,015.0	15.95
1979	80.90	359	297,543	1,322	2,563.3	11.6	5,173.4	15.64
1980	78.12	344	[R]373,790	[R]1,645	2,789.5	13.4	5,161.7	15.13
1981	76.17	332	[R]427,140	[R]1,861	3,128.4	13.7	5,291.7	14.39
1982	73.15	316	[R]425,703	[R]1,838	3,255.0	13.1	5,189.3	14.10
1983	73.04	312	[R]416,670	[R]1,782	3,536.7	11.8	5,423.8	13.47
1984	[R]76.72	325	[R]434,367	[R]1,842	3,933.2	[R]11.0	5,813.6	13.20
1985	76.49	[R]322	[R]437,517	[R]1,839	4,220.3	10.4	6,053.7	12.64
1986	76.76	320	[R]382,861	[R]1,594	4,462.8	8.6	6,263.6	12.25
1987	[R]79.18	327	[R]396,082	[R]1,635	4,739.5	8.4	6,475.1	12.23
1988	82.82	339	[R]409,989	[R]1,677	5,103.8	8.0	6,742.7	12.28
1989	[R]84.95	344	[R]437,160	[R]1,771	5,484.4	8.0	6,981.4	12.17
1990	84.65	339	[R]472,030	[R]1,891	5,803.1	8.1	7,112.5	11.90
1991	84.61	334	[R]470,095	[R]1,858	5,995.9	7.8	7,100.5	11.92
1992	85.96	335	[R]475,069	[R]1,852	6,337.7	7.5	7,336.6	11.72
1993	[R]87.61	337	[R]490,624	[R]1,888	6,657.4	7.4	7,532.7	11.63
1994	89.26	339	[R]503,693	[R]1,914	7,072.2	7.1	7,835.5	11.39
1995	91.17	342	[R]513,587	[R]1,929	7,397.7	6.9	8,031.7	11.35
1996	[R]94.18	350	[R]559,455	[R]2,077	7,816.9	7.2	8,328.9	11.31
1997	94.77	348	[R]566,277	[R]2,077	8,304.3	6.8	8,703.5	10.89
1998	95.18	345	[R]525,285	[R]1,904	8,747.0	6.0	9,066.9	10.50
1999	96.82	347	[R]556,052	[R]1,993	9,268.4	6.0	9,470.3	10.22
2000	98.98	351	[R]688,774	[R]2,441	9,817.0	7.0	9,817.0	10.08
2001	96.33	338	[R]693,897	2,434	10,128.0	6.9	9,890.7	9.74
2002	97.86	340	[R]661,496	[R]2,299	10,469.6	6.3	10,048.8	9.74
2003	98.21	338	[R]754,147	[R]2,599	10,960.8	6.9	10,301.0	9.53
2004	100.35	[R]343	[R]868,595	[R]2,966	11,685.9	7.4	10,675.8	9.40
2005	[R]100.48	340	[R]1,044,898	[R]3,535	[R]12,421.9	8.4	[R]10,989.5	[R]9.14
2006	[R]99.88	[R]335	[R]1,157,910	[R]3,881	[R]13,178.4	[R]8.8	[R]11,294.8	[R]8.84
2007	[R]101.55	337	NA	NA	[R]13,807.5	NA	[R]11,523.9	[R]8.81
2008[P]	99.30	327	NA	NA	14,264.6	NA	11,652.0	8.52

Sources: **Energy Consumption:** Table 1.3. **Energy Expenditures:** Table 3.5. **Gross Domestic Product:** Table D1. **Population Data: Other Columns:** Calculated by EIA.

ARTHUR JACKSON

Complexity, Population density, and Energy

Mankind has moved from a society of hunters and gatherers to one of stability produced by new methods of food production created from farming. This created stability, but did not provide the dynamic growth that we would see in the latter parts of the 18th century. This would come from industrialization, and the resultant increase in population densities brought about by urban complexes. These complexes are not only the melting pots of our society, they create the sophistication, and complexity that our Society thrives upon and grows from. Urban centers are being created at an ever-increasing rate in modern society. Some of these are official, being created by governments in the form of structured organized cities, where many others are unofficial, being created by hardship, deprivation, and hunger. As a matter of record, we often create these unofficial pockets of urbanization as a way of dealing with the economic deprivation of one culture or another. Whatever the method of creation, urban centers marked an increasing complexity in social evolution. The study a population density in urban complexes is not new. In 1998 Joseph Tainter wrote a book identifying the relationship between this factor and energy. Where we have

144

large concentrations of population, or high population densities we have a growing complex of problems. The solution of each problem will create new levels of complexity. Complexity as a concept can be defined as follows:

> Complexity is generally understood to refer to such things as the size of a society, the number and distinctiveness of its parts, the variety of specialized social roles that it incorporates, the number of distinct social personalities present, and the variety of mechanisms for organizing these into a coherent, functioning whole. Augmenting any of these dimensions increases the complexity of a society. Hunter-gatherer societies (by way of illustrating one contrast in complexity) contain no more than a few dozen distinct social personalities, while modern European censuses recognize 10,000 to 20,000 unique occupational roles, and industrial societies may contain overall more than 1,000,000 different kinds of social personalities (McGuire 1983; Tainter 1988).

From: **GETTING DOWN TO EARTH:** Practical Applications of Ecological Economics, Island Press, 1996; ISBN 1-55963-503-7 http://www.amazon.com/exec/obidos/ASIN/1559635037

In the early stages of human evolution as we moved from hunter-gatherer's, humanity evolved into low density foragers and finally into low density early farming communities. But humanity has an ability to become complex, and perhaps, in a sense even seeks growing complexity. The industrial revolution provided the spark needed to create urban complexes which would be the incubators from growing social and technological complexity. In today's world complexity is a given. As I often remind my students, the average person in the modern world has a growing need for technology, and the data that it controls. We run our lives on the basis of information. In order to provide that information we need very complex and sophisticated systems. With each of the systems there is an equally complex support network. With this complexity we seek constraints on human behavior, and place growing burdens on time and energy. Problem-solving is an energy intense operation. Each time we undertake a complex problem the result and solution requires the expenditures of growing amounts of energy. As more and more urban centers evolve complexity will increase, and so will the need for energy to meet the growing demands of complexity and problem-solving. As we can see in table 17 urban complexes in the United States will continue to increase in size, and resultant population density.

Table 17 Total Population, Population Change, and Population Ranking for the Ten Largest Cities
in the United States: 1900 to 2000

area	1900	1910	1920	1930	1940	1950	1960	1970	1980	1990	2000
United States	75,994,575	91,972,266	105,710,620	122,775,046	131,669,275	150,697,361	179,323,175	203,211,926	226,545,805	248,709,873	281,421,90
Total population,	9,477,400	12,401,322	15,355,850	19,042,823	19,906,825	21,729,384	21,751,334	22,028,346	20,886,343	21,872,554	23,899,236
Percent .	12.5	13.5	14.5	15.5	15.1	14.4	12.1	10.8	9.2	8.8	8.5
New York	3,437,202	4,766,883	5,620,048	6,930,446	7,454,995	7,891,957	7,781,984	7,894,862	7,071,639	7,322,564	8,008,278
Chicago	1,698,575	2,185,283	2,701,705	3,376,438	3,396,808	3,620,962	3,550,404	3,366,957	3,005,072	2,783,726	2,896,016
Philadelphia	1,293,697	1,549,008	1,823,779	1,950,961	1,931,334	2,071,605	2,002,512	1,948,609	1,688,210	1,585,577	1,517,550
St Louis	575,238	687,029	772,897	821,960	816,048	856,796	750,026	x	x	x	x
Boston	560,892	670,585	748,060	781,188	770,816	801,444	x	x	x	x	x
Baltimore	508,957	558,485	733,826	804,874	859,100	949,708	939,024	905,759	786,775	x	x
Cleveland	381,768	560,663	796,841	900,429	878,336	914,808	876,050	750,903	x	x	x
Buffalo	352,387	423,715	x	x	x	x	x	x	x	x	x
San Francisco	342,782	x	x	x	x	x	x	x	x	x	x
Cincinnati	325,902	x	x	x	x	x	x	x	x	x	x

X Not applicable.
Note: Population, change from previous decade, and ranking shown only for censuses when the city ranked among the ten largest in the United States.
Source: U.S. Census Bureau, decennial census of population, 1900 to 2000.

147

As seen in table 18 the energy consumption per capita will continue to increase in accordance with population density in urban centers. This exchange between complexity and energy creates a new concern for modern society; potential collapse.

Table 18 *Energy and Resources — Energy Consumption: Total energy consumption per capita*
Units: Kilograms of oil equivalent (kgoe) per person

World	1,668.0	1,657.0	1,778.0

Region/Classification	1990	2000	2005
Asia (excluding Middle East)	775.8	865.2	1,051.5
Central America & Caribbean	1,243.1	1,266.3	1,365.9
Europe	4,080.4	3,580.8	3,773.4
Middle East & North Africa	1,184.6	1,531.5	1,765.5
North America	7,686.3	8,157.9	7,942.9
South America	970.1	1,123.8	1,151.2
Developed Countries	4,755.8	4,622.6	4,720.0
Developing Countries	684.6	807.5	975.9
High Income Countries	4,906.0	5,468.7	5,523.6
Low Income Countries	431.5	457.3	491.8
Middle Income Countries	1,365.4	1,252.9	1,509.3

International Energy Agency (IEA) Statistics Division. 2007. *Energy Balances of OECD Countries (2008 edition)* and *Energy Balances of Non-OECD Countries (2007 edition)*. Paris: IEA. Available at http://data.iea.org/ieastore/default.asp.

Food , Energy , and Water

The study of collapse has become a major concern for modern societies. History is replete with empires, and societies that have been complex, and sophisticated, in modern terms, and reached a point of collapse. What we may need to consider is whether the term collapse is truly appropriate; whether we're simply looking at systems, that are very sophisticated, and synchronous, that may simply have moved to another mode of complexity. The question is whether collapse occurs, or whether we simply have a new system evolve. One such look at this phenomenon was discussed by Steven Strogatz in his book, "Sync the Emerging Science of Spontaneous Order" in which he examines the evolution of Systems from growing complexity. Does any system ever die, or does it evolve it a more complex version of itself? This is perhaps something that scientists will be arguing over for many generations to come. Yet it is clear that human interaction in dense population groups creates growing issues that need to be resolved, while providing the concentration of intellect we need to solve problems. We can consider the factors of disease and its control as one parameter that creates an ever increasing need to analyze and study how human populations interact with each other, and moved in these new and ever changing complex structures. In today's world we know that there is a growing need for interconnection because of data transfer. Technology has created a growing need for more and more data as exemplified in Moore's Law. But, will this data concentration be able to offset the problems it creates. The growing need for energy will also create increasing disputes as we see the emergence of urban centers outside of the developed world.

Developing countries are racing quickly to catch up with the developed world of Europe and America in terms of sophistication. The result of this is an ever-increasing number of urban centers that are growing in number and in size. As exhibited in table 19 we see the growth of a selected number of urban centers over time.

Table 19 *POPULATION OF CITIES WITH 10 MILLION* INHABITANTS OR MORE, 1950, 1975, 2001 AND 2015

(millions)

1950			1975			2001			2015		
	city	population		city	population		city	population		city	population
1	New York	12.3	1	Tokyo	9.8	1	Tokyo	26.5	1	Tokyo	27.2
			2	New York	15.9	2	Sao Palo	18.3	2	Dhaka	22.8
			3	Shanghai	11.4	3	Mexico City	18.8	3	Mumbai	22.6
			4	Mexico City	10.7	4	New York	16.8	4	Sao Palo	21.2
			5	Sao Palo	10.3	5	Mumbai	16.5	5	Delhi	20.9
						6	Los Angeles	13.3	6	Mexico City	20.4
						7	Calcutta	13.3	7	New York	17.9
						8	Dhaka	13.2	8	Jakarta	17.3
						9	Delhi	13.0	9	Calcutta	16.7
						10	Shanghai	12.8	10	Karachi	16.2
						11	Buenos Aires	12.1	11	Lagos	16.0
						12	Jakarta	11.4	12	Los Angles	14.5
						13	Osaka	11.0	13	Shanghai	13.6
						14	Beijing	10.8	14	Buenos Aires	13.2
						15	Rio de Janeiro	10.8	15	Metro Manila	12.6
						16	Karachi	10.4	16	Beijing	11.7
						17	Metro Manila	10.1	17	Rio de Janeiro	11.5
									18	Cairo	11.5
									19	Istanbul	11.4
									20	Osaka	11.0
									21	Tianjin	10.3

Source: United Nations Population Division, *World Urbanization Prospects: The 2001 Revision.*

Urbanization is having its greatest impact outside of the developed world. Developing countries are creating more urban centers, larger urban centers, with a greater degree of complexity than in the developed world. This process will only continue as urban centers are magnets for the young, energetic, and the desperate of our society. These centers are where education, entertainment, and just about any other thing that you can imagine will be found. The energy that is needed to fuel the centers and to solve the problems that they will engender will only increase exponentially. We've already begun to tap new sources from coal, wind, and the emerging energy sources of nuclear fuel and green technology. Will this be enough to meet the growing demand of urban complexes and their complexity? Only time will tell. Yet, humanity will not stop developing urban complexes. They are fundamental to the very nature of human society and are critical to the survival of such societies.

Although there are many books about the collapse of civilizations as they grew beyond their ability to control and satisfied the needs of the complex societies within them, they did not cease to exist but continued through the imprints they left on modern society; imprints that will never fade. Rome may no longer be an empire, but its impact on the modern world is seen in the laws, society, and technology of today. The greatest achievements of Rome were not its armies, but its engineering skill. Likewise we see those same contributions being passed on from other civilizations in terms of science, music, art, culture, and social organization. It is an interesting question to consider what the future world will look like as more and more urban centers are created outside of North America and Europe.

ARTHUR JACKSON

Complexity and wealth

Complexity is a concentrator of energy, and wealth. It creates inequality. This pressure to try and equalize systems by spreading energy and technology brings the developing countries into conflict with the Western democracies. To allow uncontrolled and unfettered access to the technologies that would bring these masses of people into the marketplace would do irreparable harm to the Democratic economies, or so it was believed. As always, there was the increasing need for security. China is desperately seeking technology. India, the world's largest democracy, with a population rivaling that of China, has a great need to obtain technology to move it into the modern world. Yet, what is provided by the developed nations is often limited by the continuing needs of national security and competition. Despite these restrictions, developing nations are creating wealth at an explosive rate. In table 20 we can see how wealth is being redistributed by this new pressure to compete.

Table 20 WEALTH IN THE 20TH CENTURY

Year	Percentage of wealth held by top 1% of the population	Percentage of wealth held by top 10% of the population	Percentage of wealth held by top 50% of the population
1911	70%	---	---
1914	---	---	---
1919	66%	---	---
1922	---	---	---
1926/28	60%	---	---
1936	55%	---	---
1954	43%	80%	
1960	---	---	---
1066	33%	69%	97%
1971	31%	65%	97%
1976	24%	60%	95%
1980	20%	52%	94%

Source: Inland Revenue www.inlandrevenue.gov.uk - this includes housing and financial wealth.

Wealth brings with it the need for information to protect that wealth and to generate more. Today's societies face a new type of complexity with the ever-increasing requirement for more and more data to be made available to the average citizen. The Internet makes it possible for people to obtain growing amounts of information from various sources at increasing speeds. The principle of Moore's Law is directly applicable to the increased density of microprocessors, increase speed, and memory requirements. This process brings about a number of complex issues for societies. The ever present need for security and protection of each nation's citizens faces new and direct challenges as the Internet will become the battleground of the future.

Cyber warfare is already taking a prominent position in the thinking of military analyst and business leaders as they look at the world of tomorrow and try to determine the most vulnerable areas for their operations. More importantly, this new complexity brings the world together in an ever growing level of interconnectivity. The need of each and every citizen to be able to engage in communication, data collection, cultural exchange, or entertainment enterprise the individuals on a global basis is expected as today's norm. Each of these changes brings with it a corresponding increase in energy requirements. Households today, whether they're in the developed world, or the developing world, have a growing need for this interconnectivity. This requires the creation of new types of infrastructures to support data transfer. Along with this infrastructure comes the need for newer and faster systems to handle the increasing data demands. In addition to these issues requirements will increase in cultural needs as society struggles to cope with the new types of information that it must assess.

In today's world we can already see the differences in technological awareness between members of the Baby boom generation, the X and Y generations and millennial generations. Members of the millennial, and X and Y generations were born into a world of technological connectedness, and are therefore more comfortable than boomers. In countries such as China, India, Brazil, and Russia, with large numbers of millennial and x and y generations in their populations, we see an expansion of these systems in ways, and in intensity that had not been expected. In China and India, they race to take advantage of this new technology to move into a new era of educational awareness, as they begin to train large numbers of scientists, engineers, and managers for the new applications in technology. Russia, although no longer a dominant competitor, is likewise making massive strides to develop capabilities in this area. As each of these efforts takes root, there is a growing competition for the resources that will make it possible for these governments to meet their needs in technology, as well as more traditional areas of energy requirements.

These new energy requirements result in increased competition for not only traditional resources such as coal, and oil, but new resources such as magnetic generation, tidal energy, new generations of solar cells, and ultimate fusion technology. Early work to develop prototypes and experimental models in these new technologies is already well under way. We will see increasing effort to expand research and development for new types of energy systems in the future. The exact form and nature of the systems is yet to be defined.

This brings into question one of the key concepts of collapse theory. Societies may, although not necessarily reach a point where there are diminishing returns on Education and Research, and ultimately fail. Sometimes that change is predictable and controllable, and other times it is chaotic, unpredictable, and uncontrolled. Looking through the prism of time, 70 years ago established models would not have allowed for the existence of complex synchronous systems that exist in so many areas of society today. The existence of fractals, small world complexes, advanced systems analysis, cyber technology, and a growing Internet are all new and unexpected ways of adjusting to growing human complexity and urban density. Problem solving societies are just as unpredictable in the nature of the responses they will have to these challenges, as are the challenges themselves. The larger the resultant population density, the greater are the number of alternatives available to humanity to deal with these problems. Complexity creates the chaotic mixtures that will ultimately result in new ordered systems with new and unique solutions.

Food production and its associated systems are moving toward complexity by reducing the number of species used within the system, and by making the remainder more complex through genetic manipulation. For energy, we increase the number and complexity of sources in the process, to create new complexities and new answers to these complexities. Two critical pillars of our social system are operating in opposition to each other. In that regard, they both require the same commodity to survive; water.

ARTHUR JACKSON

Water: The critical component

Food , Energy , and Water

Our planet has an abundance of water. It has helped to shape the surface of the planet, as well as the habitat, habits, and social structures of the creatures that reside on the surface of land. But, water is more than a simple liquid. The oceans, the primary source of water on this planet are a prime mover in the creation of climate through the flow of thermal energy in the ocean currents. Oceans are prime generators of temperature moderation in Europe and in North America. The oceans play a fundamental part in the distribution of heat throughout the planet's surface. They also are the prime incubator for most of the life on the planet. All life on this planet began in the oceans. Yet, there are other ways water adds to the social and geological structure of our planet as well.

The cycle of evaporation and condensation from oceans, lakes, rivers, and streams provides the rainfall that helps to nurture landmasses all around the globe. The water cycle is a fundamental part of life on this planet. It nurtures our societies, and all the species of the planet. The earliest human civilizations, hunter gatherers, were dependent upon water sources for their survival. Where there was water, there was an abundance of plant life, and animal life with the substance of survival. As humanity has progressed from an agricultural environment to one of industrialization, water plays an ever more important part.

ARTHUR JACKSON

Industrialization would not have been possible without the existence of water sources to feed the engines of Industry that evolved out of the industrial revolution. Rivers and lakes were the primary means of transportation for goods and services produced by these urban centers. They formed the nucleus of the earliest forms of urban transportation systems. One need only look a global map to see cities evolving along rivers or at the junction of rivers as transport water ways, sources of water for domestic use, for industrial use, and for farming. Even today modern Metroplexes are always located in conjunction to critical sources of water. The growth of human societies has produced an increasing amount of stress on the available water sources of this planet. This pressure will increase with time.

In today's world conflicts often erupt over the existence of and the relocation of water sources. In modern societies the growing amounts of water needed to balance the growing competition between agricultural needs, industrial needs, and domestic needs for cities and people is increasing exponentially. As developing countries begin their march toward equalization with the developed countries of America and Europe, competition for the resource becomes more pronounced as new countries require larger quantities of water for humans, agricultural use, and industrialization. In keeping

162

with the nature of human societies, and the complexity of human interactions, we will see a growing competition for these resources between states, nations, and regions of the globe. Geopolitical politics will play an increasingly important part in water distribution in the future. The United Nations since 2000 has been engaged in a series of studies and programs to encourage nations to engage in a structured and orderly development and protection of water resources on the planet. This effort has been joined in recent years by a number organizations concerned with the growing impact of global warming. This new climate phenomenon has become a major consideration as water patterns across the planet have begun to realign, or shift due to the efforts of either natural forces, or human intervention. How significant this will be in the growing complexity of human urbanization only time will tell. What we do know is that it is a factor to be considered in the growing conflict between two central pillars of human society; the need for food to sustain the species, and need for energy to solve the growing complex of problems created by urbanization and rapid modernization of developing countries. Although the world is four fifths water it is often misguided to believe that there is enough water, to solve the problems of today's urban societies. As United Nations studies have shown, by the year 2030, 40% of global populations will live in water depressed areas. This means they will live in areas with not be enough water to meet their daily living needs. Looking at the abundance of the liquid across the surface of the planet people will often find this puzzling and confusing. Yet, when you look at the breakdown of water on this planet, you can understand the problem that exists. Table 21 shows one calculation of all water sources on the planet. Fresh water represents less than three percent of total global water. The rest is inaccessible, or very difficult to make available for human use.

Water source	Water volume, in cubic kilometers	% of fresh water	% of total water
Oceans, Seas, & Bays	1,338,000,000	--	96.5
Ice caps, Glaciers, & Permanent Snow	24,064,000	68.7	1.74
Groundwater	23,400,000	--	1.7
Fresh	10,530,000	30.1	0.76
Saline	12,870,000	--	0.94
Soil Moisture	16,500	0.05	0.001
Ground Ice & Permafrost	300,000	0.86	0.022
Lakes	176,400	--	0.013
Fresh	91,000	0.26	0.007
Saline	85,400	--	0.006
Atmosphere	12,900	0.04	0.001
Swamp Water	11,470	0.03	0.0008
Rivers	2,120	0.006	0.0002
Biological Water	1,120	0.003	0.0001
Total	1,386,000,000	-	100

Table 21 Water calculation—
Source: Igor Shiklomanov chapter "World fresh water resources" in Peter H. Gleick's (editor), 1993, Water in Crisis: A Guide to the World's Fresh Water Resources (Oxford University Press, New York).

ARTHUR JACKSON

More than 96 percent of all water on this planet is salt water. Salt water cannot be used for human consumption. However, it can be converted, at great expense into fresh water. Today many countries in the Middle East, and other parts of the world are turning to desalinization plants as a way of producing the supply of fresh water that they need. One such method called reverse osmosis. Although promising, its costs are very high averaging over $1,000 per acre foot of water to be desalinated. For many poor countries this would make it too expensive for them to use. For the oil rich countries of the Middle East, with billions of dollars of excess capital, this amount of expense, and energy is a reasonable alternative. Desalinization is one of the oldest forms of water treatment known to man. In its basic form it is really a system of filtration which removes salt and leaves fresh water. In today's world 75% or all the desalination plants in operation are in the Middle East. Yet desalination brings with it another unique problem, damage to the ocean themselves. As salt water is removed the saline content in the remaining body of water tend to increase in salinity, becoming what is called brine. Concentrations of water with high salt content make it difficult for marine species to survive.

Food , Energy , and Water

Another source of difficult to reach water is the ice caps. Here again the source of water does not present the same problem as desalinization, but presents its own unique problem. Movement of large quantities of polar icecaps may have a disastrous impact on global climate. The polar caps tend to be sources of weather generation, and temperature moderation. There is also the unique problem of moving polar ice to locations where it may be needed. This requires huge amounts of energy for the relocation of the ice, the melting of the ice, and the pumping of water to locations where it will be needed. Whenever we begin to address these difficult problems we run into the continual conflict between agricultural systems and energy systems. The growth of human populations requires we increase food production using genetically engineered materials if population needs are to be met. The movement of ice bergs solves a problem but brings with it a complex series of problems associated with the solution. The first of these problems is evaporation. This is a problem that has been evolving since the creation of the industrial complex. As we can see in table 22 water usage for industrial and domestic consumption will increase significantly, but so will evaporation for global populations through the year 2010. Since most industrial complexes use reservoirs' as holding facilities for the water, we must also be concerned with a resultant evaporation of water from those sources. As seen from table 22, the growth in water consumption from these two sources will be significant. In table 23 we show projections in the increases in water consumption for selected countries around the globe in agriculture, industrial, and in a simple and domestic use projected to the year 2013. From this table you can see that developing countries or moving large quantities of water out of agriculture in into industrial applications as they work to catch up with the developed countries in technology. You can see the figure for China shows a swing away from agricultural production toward industrial applications. India still has a very large commitment to agriculture with a growing commitment to industrial applications. As indicated in the table the projection for this growth is relatively small. But note the figures for Europe and North America as they move more and more of their water into industrial applications and less of that to agricultural. As urbanization and makes its way through Asia and gradually begins to impact parts of India, which will see a continual struggle between the allocation of water resources for agriculture, industry, and human consumption. The major struggle will be between agriculture and industry. To understand how this will develop we need to look at several cases dealing with these two areas to show how nations are moving to meet these allocations and some of the

Food , Energy , and Water

consequences of those efforts. We will look at Russian efforts
in the Aral sea, which has resulted in an unprecedented change
in that sea, and in the United States at the problems of cities
such as Los Angles and Atlanta to maintain water sources for
their industries and people. We will then look at industrial water
usage as it impacts developing countries, in particular, China.

Table 22 Industrial and Domestic Consumption
Compared with Evaporation from reservoirs

years	Industrial and domestic consumption km³	Evaporation from reservoirs km³
1900	25	10
1940	40	15
1950	51	27
1960	80	75
1970	110	130
1980	125	160
1990	130	190
1995	145	205
2000	175	240
2010	248	270

Source: Igor Shiklomanov's, State Hydrological Institute
and United nations Educational, Scientific, and Cultural Organization 1999

Table 23 Projected Increase in Demand from 2005-2030

Billion M^3

	Agriculture	Industrial	Municipal and Domestic	
China	178	300	54	
India	338	89	40	
Sub-Saharan Africa	320	28	92	
Asia	243	117	80	
N. America	181	124	21	
Europe	72	100	12	
S. America	89	68	23	
Mena	85	9	6	
Oceania	21	7	x	

Source:
Economic frameworks to inform decision-making
Charting Our Water Future 2009, http://www.ifc.org/ifcext/southasia.nsf/AttachmentsByTitle/waterreport/$FILE/Charting_Our_Water_Future_Full_Report_001.pdf

Modern Agriculture and Water

The Aral Sea was a fresh water body formed by a depression sometime between 26,000,00 and 2.6 Million years ago. The depression became filled with rain water and the runoff from to rivers, Sry Drya, and the Amu Drya. The climate across the sea was characterized by wide ranging temperatures from cold winters to hot summers as well as sparse rainfall. Precipitation in this region averages 4 in., or 100 mm annual. This is only a tiny fraction of what was needed in order to maintain its water levels. The input from the two rivers was critical to the survival of the sea. In the early 1900's to the 1960's, the surface of the sea was some 175 ft. above sea level, and covered an area of 26,300 square miles, or roughly 68,000 square kilometers. It reached from north to south was 270 mi. It extended from east to west just over 180 mi.. The boundaries of the Sea were set by Kazakhstan in the north, and Uzbekistan in South. The name Aral Sea translates to mean, "Sea of Islands", referring to the over 1500 islands dotted throughout the sea. From the 1800's to the 1900's fishing villages were located along the shores of this inland sea and were very prosperous. This was the fourth largest inland sea in the world.

ARTHUR JACKSON

As the Soviet Union came into existence in the 19th century, the new government looked at the source of water flowing into the sea as a potential source of irrigation. The diversion of these rivers would make it possible to grow rice, melons, cereals, and most importantly cotton. Cotton was considered a major import for the Soviet Union because it would produce ready cash. The goal was to divert much of the water to Kazakhstan and Uzbekistan to enable farmers to produce these crops. After much discussion and engineering evaluations construction began on series of canals to divert the water from the two principal rivers in 1940. One of the canal used for this purpose was the Qaraqum Canal. The Qaraqum Canal was the largest in central Asia at that time. However the construction methods used were of inferior quality and resulted in losses and leaks of about 75 percent of all water transported by the canal. Even today only 12 percent of this large canal is waterproof to prevent leakage.

By the 1960's, more water was taken from the rivers for irrigation than was allowed to reach the sea for replenishing the water levels in the sea. By the 1970's the sea level had fallen at a rate of almost 20 cm a year, finally reaching an astounding 50 to 60 cm per year and an all-time high of 80 to 90 cm a year by the 1980's. Despite these drastic drops in level, the water diverted from the sea for irrigation provided a successful agricultural industry throughout the region. Today Uzbekistan is a world leader in cotton production. The resultant drop in level all along the sea brought to an end the fishing industry along its shores which employed over 40,000 workers and produced almost 1/6 of the Soviet fish catch yearly. Soviet engineers had anticipated this and had expected the level of the sea to drop. It was part of their overall five-year plan. As a result the service of this sea shrank by 60 percent and lost 80 percent of its volume. Where once fishing fleets sailed across a shallow sea, there was dust and sand. The surviving portions of the sea are heavy with salinity. Salt levels are approaching those of the Dead Sea.

The shrinkage has split the remaining portion of the lake into two bodies of water which are now called the North Aral sea, and the South Aral sea. Although there has been some inflow from subsurface water into the sea it has had little impact on the evaporation which continues to shrink this body of water. But the two warring nations in an effort to preserve what is left, have begun to construct dams and redirect water into the remaining portions of the sea. In an effort to provide water for geopolitical reasons, an ecological disaster has been created. The efforts by neighboring countries may be too little too late to save this body of water.

This is the type of damage societies can do as we begin to see the competition between the need for cash ready agricultural crops and their demand on the water sources. Although this is an extreme example of the situation, it is not the only example.

The Colorado river in United States used to flow into Mexico to become part of a water system that once supported fishing much like that of Aral Sea. As the city of Los Angeles has continued to grow, and the farms in California have demanded more water so they can compete for agricultural dollars with other countries, the river no longer reaches Mexico. All of this flow is diverted either to farming within the state of California, or to the massive urban complex of Los Angeles. Today there are disputes between farmers and industry for this critical water source in United States. This battle will be repeated again and again as the continuing conflict between agricultural systems and energy systems continues to be waged for the prime resource they both so desperately need, water.

Food , Energy , and Water

Industry in China and water use

China is a country with over 20 percent of the global population, but only 7% of the global water resources. In its drive to become a modern nation, China is facing a serious trade-off between industrialized water usage and agricultural usage. With its economy expanding rapidly over the past few decades, the Chinese economy is growing at approximately 10%. The demand for industrial water currently uses up to 22 percent of China's total water, and with its growing industrial system this will increase to 62% in the next decade.

For developing nations, industrial output is always more valuable than agricultural. In the case of China the need to establish industrial resources is pivotal to its development into a global power. Prior to the start of World War Two Chinese industry was primitive, almost nonexistent. With a numerical population advantage many times that of Japan, the entire country was almost conquered by nation 10th it's size. After the war China began a series of programs to bring it into line with the rest of the industrialized world. It will not be until the 1980's that these programs would really get underway and began industrialization in China. But, like most developing countries technologies are hard to come by for developing nations. Countries such as United States and the nations of Europe are hesitant to make available cutting edge technology, and instead provide dated and wasteful technology at a high price. Similar to most countries in today's world, China has an abundance of coal available. Western powers eager to access the growing markets in China have made available coal technology instead of other systems which might provide clean energy. With the growth of Chinese energy demand, they bring on line several coal fired power plants each year to meet growing demand. More recently they have constructed the gigantic Three Gorges Dam to help provide hydroelectric power. But this too comes with a cost. Thousands of citizens were displaced, and millions of hectares of land were flooded to create the giant Lake. These are the trade-offs developing countries must consider as they struggle to catch up with developed countries in technology. Coal-fired plants produce pollution and damage the water table and water supplies of China. As giant hydroelectric projects provide clean fuel, they remove large amounts of arable land. China has less than 7 percent of the world's arable land with which to feed its huge population of 1.3 billion people.

China's population will exceed 1.5 billion by 2020. More than half of those people will be living in urban complexes and engage in energy intensive activities such as manufacturing.

Food , Energy , and Water

The urban populations require much more energy than their rural counterparts. China has built hundreds of new cities which come with urban industrialized activities to accommodate the growing need of its population for jobs, and better life style. This intense activity requires more water. China will soon reach the point where it will drop below the minimum level needed to sustain its population. Currently there are reports of water shortages in many of the farming areas of China. Wells are being drilled to new depths in excess of 1,000 ft. to provide subsurface water for many farming communities. With the economy expected to grow at a rate between 9 and 10%, the shift toward industrialization will take much of the surface and subsurface water for these new industries, leaving little for farm usage in this country. By one estimate most of the surface water with in China is already polluted to levels that make it unsafe to use by humans.

China has already stated its goal of becoming the largest user of hydroelectric power in the world. Yet, these large projects have fallen short of meeting the critical needs of the country to date. The other problem created by such projects is that they destroy large sectors of arable land reducing the already small sources for agriculture production. A recent explosion at a petroleum plant in one of the provinces created a benzene spill that flooded water supplies resulting in the evacuation of over 1 million Chinese inhabitants' and providing downstream problems for Russia, China's neighbor.

Finally as a result of climate shift changes, water scarcity will be an issue in the foreseeable future. Glaciers in Tibet are shrinking at a rate of 7 percent per year and global temperatures are expected to warm by almost one degree Celsius over the next 100 years. The warming not only causes melting of glaciers, but has caused several lakes to dry up in these regions. As China moves to shift more and more of its water resource for industrialization it faces an impending crisis in the future. Will it have enough water to feed its 1.6 billion people, and to keep them gainfully employed? We have to remember that the Chinese agricultural system is just as fragile as the global agricultural system. The number of crops that we all depend upon for food has shrunk. Although we add complexity to these products through genetic manipulation and engineering, the number is still extremely small for China and the global population. This is in contrast to the growing complexity of energy systems needed to meet industrial demand. China and India both have active nuclear programs and with the growing hydroelectric capacity will be placed in a struggle between providing food or energy for its Metroplexes.

As with all complex systems there is a clear choice between independence, and mobility. Society has a great deal of impact on the way that systems will operate by choosing one of these two options. In the early stages of humanity there was often an argument to be made about having systems that were independent. One of the early arguments was based upon Adam Smith's, Wealth of Nations, in which he chronicled the concept that strong nations must keep their resources within their borders and discourage the purchase of material produced outside of the borders. Even though there is ample historical evidence that this is not a good model, as we saw in the 1939 economic crisis, it is still an option that societies must discuss and view in terms of its impact on modern systems. Water as a fungible commodity is one of the most difficult systems to consider from this perspective. In our earlier examples we've saw how nations will often use political decisions to decide how this product should be distributed which often have very serious consequences. Yet, nations also have begun to look at water as a critical resource to be protected within their borders. This drive toward independent systems is often at odds with the natural mechanisms of complex systems which tend to be mobile and to seek stable exchanges between the neighboring systems.

The nature of complex systems is to move toward mobility and stable exchange rather than independence. Because societies are structured toward trade, water as a commodity, and a system will move in the same direction. The flow of this commodity across boundaries between nations, as between the United States and Mexico over the water from the Colorado River, or the distribution of water in the AraL Lakes in Russia, is the mobility required as the system redistributes water throughout the planet based upon complex mechanisms. In addition to this we see redistribution of water sources around a planet in response to societal systems created by humans for trade. Water is the most highly sought after and the most often traded commodity on the planet. In any product from human beings to electronics, a significant portion will be water. There has been a growing discussion over the last decade about the use of virtual water, or embedded water in manufactured products. This also applies to water as it is contained in human beings and in agricultural products which are moved about the planet. When human populations were less than 1 million, or even 1 billion persons, discussions of imbedded water sources would be nominal. Today, with 6.7 billion inhabitants on the face of the planet, and all of the products and support systems they require as they move about the globe, a discussion of imbedded water sources is vitally important. As societies become more mobile, so does this commodity. For the system of water on this planet the question becomes whether or not we can establish a stable exchange rate between countries as we move water, and imbedded water about the globe. We must also consider the impact of growing complexity up on the system.

Complex systems are affected by applications of technology. Water is no different. As societies have grown in number and complexity based upon the evolution of urban centers, so has the complex nature of their use of water. As we saw with the principle of Moores Law for computer applications, the same principles will apply to systems of food generation, energy generation, and water. All of technology has a heavy reliance upon water, and the complexity of water systems is severely impacted by the growing needs and complexity of technology. As more urban centers create new and challenging areas of complexity, we will see the need for new and ever more complex systems to provide adequate water to the cities in the future. We will also see continuous struggle to balance the needs for water between human consumption, agricultural use for food, and energy use to power the complex systems that society needs to address the ever more complex problems that they face. Once again the answer to the problem evolves out of the problem itself. Complex centers will give us the critical mass in thinking in talent and in resources to attack and solve these growing complex problems. Already we concede very ingenious applications being used to address these issues for new ways of water reclamation, to new methods of desalinization being applied around the globe. In Colorado in United States their systems in place where water is being rejected into ground locations and forced to filter through soil and sediment at a more rapid rate to aid the process of cleaning and to make usable for human consumption. Will also seen in new and innovative approaches coming out of China as that nation will be working to develop new methods of cleaning up its water supply to make it more usable for agriculture, industry, and for human consumption. We will see that this need will drive the development of systems along the same pathway as we discussed earlier for computers.

Food , Energy , and Water

Complexity and Population Density

The systems we have reviewed throughout this text are the three primary systems that govern our society. These three systems provide us with the stability, the complexity, and diversity we need, and have needed to move away from such systems as the Malthus trap and to a stable future. With the first system that we examined, that of food, we saw how mankind began its movement away the from natural diversity to create a system which would serve the needs of ever growing populations in ever more complex settings known as urban centers. Although we have moved through a period of selective exclusion, in limiting the types and numbers of plants and animals that we depend upon for food, we have added a great degree of complexity and diversity through the use of technology. The green revolution which came into existence in the 1960s made it possible for us to create a wide variety of genetically engineered materials for use as food sources. We see the process repeated with a second system ,energy as we moved into the industrial revolution. Although we begin with a limited number of energy sources, we became much more diverse and complex in the use of systems of energy as we have evolved. Finally, with water we see the primal commodity of this planet being used in ever more complex ways to serve

183

the needs of society. For all of the systems we begin to see two fundamental rules that apply to these very complex and sophisticated systems. These rules will always be in place and will continue to govern for these systems into the foreseeable future.

The rule ,which was developed by a Canadian economist to describe currency exchange in the 1960s, also applies to these fundamental systems. For each of the systems we will have two choices available. There will always be a driving effort to try to create independent systems. Independent systems by their very nature limit the exchange and transfer of information between other societies and other perspectives of political, social, or cultural needs. This limit always provides difficulties for the system to survive long-term. Independent systems, while politically desirable, are not feasible. If that is the case why do we continue to seek independence in such applications as food production, energy production, or water control. Independent systems by their very nature take away the very tools that we need to solve the growing complex problems of the future.

The other side of the coin is that we will try to make these systems mobile with a stable exchange rate between individual cultures for the exchange of information common technologies, and differing perspectives. Will we favor these

Mobile systems that provide for an exchange between diverse cultures create and you levels of complexity which drive the society forward. It is true these complexities create problems, but in addressing those problems we find new, complex, and the unique solutions which expand both our grasp of the universe, and our perspective. As we have learned to manipulate these fundamentals systems to serve the needs of ever larger populations, we've seen the evolution of the urban complex, as a place where human densities create the right environment for developing new solutions to problems as they arise. Complexity is a double edged sword. But, it is the only tool available to help mankind survive as we move forward in a more dynamic an ever changing universe of problems.

The second factor is that of population density as first establish by Moore, and applied to the growing density of components on computer chips in 1965. As societies have continued to grow, population density behaves in the same way as with digital circuitry; greater density requires and creates a exponential level of complexity. In the case of computers we have an observation which leases to understand that the density of components on a computer chip will double in density every 24 months. This rule has proved to be fundamentally true for digital systems. Whether it is a self fulfilling prophecy, since manufacturers in accepting the rule

ARTHUR JACKSON

mobile systems that tend to adhere to the principle, and determine through observation whether it is an accurate representation or observation of the way such systems evolve we may perhaps never know. Likewise, for human societies we're beginning to see population densities began to obey a similar rule to that of digital chips. As society has become larger and more complex, we see the emergence of urban centers with increased population density as a necessary and vital tool to meet the challenges of the future. These urban centers are incubators of ideas, and perspectives that are developing at a rate which is consistent with that for computer chips. This process will continue as humanity moves forward in the creation of ever greater population centers, with larger and more significant population densities. These urban centers become the laboratories that help us define new perspectives, and provide a critical mass of human ingenuity, and intellect to resolve the problems of the future. The centers are not only the cultural Mecca's of our society, but are also their technological Mecca.

These rules govern the primary systems of our society and have already been recognized at least to some degree by researchers who developed the concept of planetary boundaries. The introduction of planetary boundaries as stable areas that must be maintained by society in order to create a stable living environment that developed by a group of researchers led by Johan Rockstrom. In their research they concluded that humanity had already transgressed three of these boundaries. Most notable was the boundary which impacted biodiversity. This has long been an area of contention in its effect on the stability of human survival. The results of the loss of bio-diversity is a boundary that they maintain humanity cannot sustain. Once again we see the impact of human systems on a global scale. However dire the impact of planetary boundaries may be, it must always be balanced with the ability of humans to address and resolve the problem in unique ways.

In 2010, Craig Venter and his research group at the Venter institute reported that they had developed the first computer generated genes segment. The last barrier to human survival may be coming to an end, as we see human technology approach the issue of lack of diversity in a unique way. The use of technology to be able to create biologically diverse genetic material with the application of Computer Technology will be the new dawn of the second industrial revolution. It may bring forth the solution to the ultimate problem that humanity has faced since it began its long march away from natural diversity over 10,000 years ago. Using system such as this will we be able to create a new type of diversity based upon the needs of human societies and not at the slow and often unpredictable pace of evolution?

Notes

Food section

Ice Age

1. The early study in the movement of ice sheets has provided a wealth of information about how plants, and animals have come to inhabit certain areas of the globe, and not others. The work by people such as Godfrey Hewitt in his article, " The Genetic Legacy of the Quaternary Ice Ages" provide invaluable insight into the influence of climate change on human societies.
2. We will need to consider for some time the growing body of evidence of how the impact of changes in climate have impacted human societies.

Hunter Gatherers

1. It is not success that drives us forward, but failure. The earliest hunter-gatherers would have been stable in their system, and thus successful. These groups would have no reason to seek alternative methods of survival. Only the groups in failure or very close to failure as hunter-gatherers would be forced to seek a new way of life. History is littered with examples of this premise.

2. The exhaustion of land by continuous harvesting of wild grains would be pivotal. This was the primary motivation for a group to relocate, taking with them the system evolving from these wild fields. It is this process that shaped the size and nature of early farms. It determined the number of people that could be moved easily, and that were necessary to re-establish the system. The ability to move to a new parcel of land and re-establish the system had to be easy, independent, and successful to facilitate the spread of the system.

3. We must remember the selectivity requirement of farming. All successful hunter-gatherers would have already mastered the use of selective choice in hunting and gathering. Although unsuccessful, new groups

would bring these same skills to the new Enterprise. Selection would need to be made concerning soil, location, weather, plant type, and local water sources. For the first time selection by force (use of corals or pens) or through adaptation (by imprinting of certain species) was a tool of the system.

4. The hunter gather group size would have served as a template to developing farmers, thus establishing an optimal size of early farming communities. This selection of small group size will be pivotal

5. This was not a differentiation, but a fundamental change in behavior. It involved exclusion of certain species, and promotion of others. The same would be true of animals gradually selected as part of the farming system. We must remember that farming, at least in western terms is an integrated system of plants, animals and humans.

6. The question of why the seeds of early grains deposited themselves in such abundance in the Fertile Crescent area is a cause of much speculation. Why??

7. The creation of this system of farming utilizing plants, domestic animals and humans was an independent nodal creation. That is it allowed a small group of humans to live virtually independently of other groups. Exchange between groups would occur, but it would be necessary.

8. This system would result in the complete eradication of hunter gathers in Asia, and Europe within ????

9. This system resulted in a rapid expansion of human population, selected plant populations, and domestic animal population in a matter of .

10. The genetic evidence shows us that farming spread in response to increasing population density.(See How far from the tree, article). Cavalli-Sforza postulated that if the farmers moved, they would have taken their genes with them; but if the farming habit alone was copied, it would have had no genetic consequences. What he found was a gradient of genes across Europe, fanning out from the Middle East, and the gene map almost exactly matches the archaeological map of the spread of

wheat. This is the first significant evidence of economic competition.

11. The system of hunting and gathering was a dependent system. It relied on other wild animals and wild plants for clothing and food. The development of agriculture, with domestication of plants and animals established a closed system. The farm could provide all the things necessary to support groups of people. Farming gained this independence at the expense of hunter-gatherers. Farming required control of land.

12. It must be understood as a given, that the number of any species is limited by the availability of two critical factors. Food and water. These primary factors determine the size of a population. This of course sets aside the factor of compatibility. Parents are very familiar with this concept if they have teenagers.

13. Hunter-gatherers enjoyed a reciprocal relationship within their group only. This connection did exist indirectly between the group and other independent units around them. Some animals might have followed groups of humans to feed on leftover scraps, but this was not an

act of reciprocation. It was purely incidental. It lacked intent. For an action to be reciprocal, it must have a mental component that establishes an intentional act. You may recognize this concept from legal doctrine. The act must be two way.

14. Many of the early civilizations began along major river systems. For example Egyptians settled along the Nile River, Harappa culture along the Indus, Chinese Empire along the Huang River and the Mesopotamian Countries along the Tigris and Euphrates rivers. The river systems provided these early civilizations with a consistent source of silt from the yearly floods and water for the crops. The silt is like a natural fertilizer, bringing new minerals to enrich the crop depleted soil. This would support the recent genetic evidence that farming spread by migration primarily. Once populations consumed prime growing locations along rivers, new farms would be located in areas that would no be so quick to be replenished. Once soil conditions deteriorated, the group would relocate looking for better conditions.

15. The system that evolved out of the Younger Dryas is understood to have changed plants from   wild   to

domestic through selection. We even recognize the change of animals in the system as being altered. It also changed humans. Now they were controlling land rather than living on it. In Europe and Asia this control of land as of small parcels and groups.

What was being inherited, in his view, was not greater intelligence — being a hunter in a foraging society requires considerably greater skill than the repetitive actions of an agricultural laborer. Rather, it was "a repertoire of skills and dispositions that were very different from those of the pre-agrarian world."

Reaction to Dr. Clark's thesis from other economic historians seems largely favorable, although few agree with all of it, and many are skeptical of the most novel part, his suggestion that evolutionary change is a factor to be considered in history.

16. Historians used to accept changes in people's behavior as an explanation for economic events, like Max Weber's thesis linking the rise of capitalism with Protestantism. But most have now swung to the economists' view that all people are alike and will respond in the same way to the same incentives. Hence

they seek to explain events like the Industrial Revolution in terms of changes in institutions, not people.

17. Armed with the chimp sequence, researchers also scanned the entire human genome for deviations from normal mutation patterns. Such deviations may reveal regions of "selective sweeps," which occur when a mutation arises in a population and is so advantageous that it spreads throughout the population within a few hundred generations and eventually becomes "normal." The researchers found six regions in the human genome that have strong signatures of selective sweeps over the past 250,000 years. One region contains more than 50 genes, while another contains no known genes and lies in an area that scientists refer to as a "gene desert." Intriguingly, this gene desert may contain elements regulating the expression of a nearby protocadherin gene, which has been implicated in patterning of the nervous system. (See A Theory of Affluence and Gene Comparison with Chimps)

18. However, the intense selection for specific phenotypic traits that occurs at the founding of a dog breed, and thereafter, may leave a genetic signal in the underlying

genome that allows the genetic basis of the trait to be determined without an extensive breeding design. Specifically, intense selection on single discrete phenotypic traits is predicted to result in reduced levels of variability in the region surrounding the gene or genes that influence the phenotypic trait.

Food , Energy , and Water

Energy

1. The economic conflict posed by energy, technology, and trade is the major one of this era. Consumption to promote economic growth has become synonymous with globalization. This conflict has reshaped the need for energy. Energy production has become captive of technology to increase outputs to meet demand. Trade drives the system. All efforts to provide control have been met with resistance from free market forces.

2. The Industrial revolution brought these independent components together into a system.

3. There are numerous examples of what un-bridled consumption can do. Think of Easter island. Think of the Mammoth hunter in Russia.

4. The industrial revolution was the starting point of the conflict between carbon energy and non-carbon energy. We have established a pattern of development that each

country must use to become global. You start with European style agriculture, proceed to Western style industrialization, and finally the Service sector economy. Each phase has now become massively energy dependent. By energy we mean carbon based energy, oil and coal.

5. Consumption has created wealth stratification in the extreme. For poor countries to catch up, they must emulate the energy consumption patterns of the developed countries.

6. The pivotal question; Do I have a right to do something simply because I can afford it, or do I have an ethical obligation to decide what I should do based on global concerns??

Water

1. The conflict here is the competition between Industry v. farming v. people.
2. Do not forget the economic conflict between genetic alteration by humans and natural alteration in nature.

ARTHUR JACKSON

Table of references

A

Ahmad, Sheikh Saeed, and Javed, Sumaira; EXPLORING THE ECONOMICVALUE OF UNDERUTILIZED PLANT SPECIES IN AYUBIA NATIONAL PARK, *Pak. J. Bot.*, 39(5): 1435-1442, 2007.

Allen, J. A.: The Influence of Physical Conditions on the Genesis of Species. *Radic Rev*, 1877. **1**: 108 -140.

Allen, Robert C; *Agricultural Productivity and Rural Incomes in England and the Yangtze Delta, c. 1620- c. 1820,* Nuffield College New Road, Oxford OX1 1NF
United Kingdom

Altieri, Miguel A.; *Modern Agriculture: Ecological impacts and the possibilities for truly sustainable farming,* http://www.cnr.berkeley.edu/~agroeco3/index.html

Ambrose, Stanley H. "*Late Pleistocene Human Population Bottlenecks*, VolcanicWinter, and the Differentiation of Modern Humans." *Journal of Human Evolution* 34 (1998): 623-651.

AmericanPublicMedia,http://americanradioworks.publicradio.or g/features/gmos_india/history.html

B

BAR-OZ, GUY. n.d. *Epipalaeolithic Subsistence Strategies in the Levant: A Zooarchaeological Perspective*. Boston: The American School of Prehistoric Research (ASPR) Monograph Series, Brill Academic Publishers
Inc. Accepted for publication, pending revision.

BARUCH, URI. 1994. "*The Late Quaternary pollen record of the Near East*" in *Late Quaternary Chronology and Palaeoclimates of the Eastern Mediterranean*. Edited by O. Bar-Yosef and R.S. Kra, pp. 103-119.
Tucson: Radiocarbon (University of Arizona).

BARUCH, URI AND SYTZE BOTTEMA. 1991. "*Palynological evidence for climatic changes in the Levant ca. 17,000-9,000*

ARTHUR JACKSON

B.P." in The Natufian Culture in the Levant. Edited by O. Bar-Yosef and F. R. Valla, pp.
11-20. Ann Arbor: International Monographs in Prehistory.

BAR-YOSEF, O. 1970. *The Epi-Palaeolithic Cultures of Palestine.* Unpublished Ph.D. Dissertation. Institute of Archaeology, Hebrew University, Jerusalem, Israel.

BAR-YOSEF, OFER. 1991. "*The archaeology of the Natufian layer at Hayonim Cave*" in The Natufian Culture in the Levant. Edited by O. Bar-Yosef and F. R. Valla, pp. 81-92. Ann Arbor: International Monographs in Prehistory.

BAR-YOSEF, OFER. 1996. "*The impact of Late Pleistocene— Early Holocene climatic changes on humans in Southwest Asia*" in Humans at the End of the Ice Age: The Archaeology of the Pleistocene-Holocene
Transition. Edited by L.G. Straus, B.V. Eriksen, J.M. Erlandson, and D.R. Yesner, pp. 61-76. New York:
Plenum Press.

.

BAR-YOSEF, OFER AND ANNA BELFER-COHEN. 2002. "*Facing environmental crisis. Societal and cultural changes at the transition from the Younger Dryas to the Holocene in the Levant*" in The Dawn of Farming in the Near East. Edited by R.T.J. Cappers and S. Bottema, pp. 55-66. Studies in Early NearEastern Production, Subsistence and Environment 6. Berlin: Ex oriente.

BAR-YOSEF, OFER AND ANNA BELFER-COHEN. n.d. "*The Natufian in Hayonim Cave and the Natufian of the Terrace*" in preparation for volume on Hayonim Terrace. Edited by F.R. Valla.

BAR-YOSEF, OFER AND AVI GOPHER. 1997. *An Early Neolithic Village in the Jordan Valley Part I: The Archaeology of Netiv Hagdud.* Cambridge: Peabody Museum of Archaeology and Ethnology, Harvard University.

BAR-YOSEF, OFER AND RICHARD H. MEADOW. 1995. "*The origins of agriculture in the Near East*" in Last Hunters-First Farmers: New Perspectives on the Prehistoric Transition to Agriculture. Edited by T. D. Price and A. B. Gebauer, pp. 39-94. Santa Fe: School of American Research Press.

BELFER-COHEN, ANNA. 1988. The Natufian Settlement at Hayonim Cave: A Hunter-gatherer Band on the Threshold of Agriculture. Unpublished Ph.D. Dissertation. Institute of Archaeology, The Hebrew University, Jerusalem.

BELFER-COHEN, ANNA. 1991. *The Natufian in the Levant.* Annual Review of Anthropology 20:167-186.

.

BELFER-COHEN, ANNA AND LEORE GROSMAN. 1997. *The lithic assemblage of Salibiya I. Mitekufa*t Haeven 27:19-42.

BELFER-COHEN, A., S.L. SCHEPARTZ, AND B. ARENSBURG. 1991. "*New biological data for the Natufian populations in Israel in the Natufian Culture in the Levant*". Edited by O. Bar-Yosef and F.R. Valla, pp. 411-424. Ann Arbor: International Monographs in Prehistory.

BETTS, ALISON V. 1987. Jebel es-Subhi: a Natufian site in eastern Jordan. Paléorient 13(1): 99-103.
BETTS, ALISON V. 1991. "The Late Epipaleolithic in the Black Desert, Eastern Jordan" in The Natufian Culture in the Levant.

Edited by O. Bar-Yosef and F.R. Valla, pp. 217-234. Ann Arbor: International Monographs in Prehistory.

Bush M.B, Silman M.R, de Toledo M.B, Listopad C, Gosling W.D, Williams C, de Oliveira P.E, Krisel C. *Holocene fire and occupation in Amazonia: records from two lake districts. Phil. Trans. R. Soc. B.* 2007;**362**:209–218. doi:10.1098/rstb.2006.1980 [PubMed]

Butchart S.H.M, Stattersfield A.J, Baillie J.E.M, Bennun L.A, Stuart S.N, Akçakaya H.R, Hilton-Taylor C, Mace G.M. *Using Red List Indices to measure progress towards the 2010 target and beyond. Phil. Trans. R. Soc. B.* 2005;**360**:255–268. doi:10.1098/rstb.2004.1583 [PubMed]

C
Carlino, Gerald, Satyajit Chatterjee, and Robert M. Hunt. 2006. *"Urban Density and the Rate of Invention."* Federal Reserve Bank of PhiladelphiaWorking Paper No. 06-14.

ARTHUR JACKSON

Caro T.M, O'Doherty G. On the use of surrogate species in conservation biology. *Conserv. Biol.* 1999;**13**:805–814. doi:10.1046/j.1523-1739.1999.98338.x

Chatterjee, Satyajit, and Gerald A. Carlino. 2001. "*Aggregate Metropolitan Employment Growth and the Deconcentration of Metropolitan Employment.*" Journal of Monetary Economics 48 (3): 549-83.

Chazdon R.L, Letcher S.G, van Breugel M, Martínez-Ramos M, Bongers F, Finegan B. Rates of change in tree communities of secondary Neotropical forests following major disturbances. *Phil. Trans. R. Soc. B.* 2007;**362**:273–289. doi:10.1098/rstb.2006.1990 [PubMed]

Ciccone, Antonio, and Robert E. Hall. 1996. "*Productivity and the Density of Economic Activity.*" American Economic Review 86 (1): 54-70.

Clark, Gregory, "*A Farewell to Alms*" Princeton University Press, 2007

D

Davis, J.M. , "*The Archaeology and animals*", Yale University Press New Haven and London, 1987

Diamond, Jared, "*Guns, Germs, and Steel: The Fates of Human Societies*", W.W. Norton and company, NewYork, 1999

E

F

FAO SYMPOSIUM ON *AGRICULTURE, TRADE AND FOOD SECURITY: ISSUES AND OPTIONS IN THE FORTHCOMING WTO NEGOTIATIONS FROM THE PERSPECTIVE OF DEVELOPING COUNTRIES*, Geneva, 23-24 September 1999

Frankham, Richard, "*Genetics and extinction*" Journal of biological conservation, volume 126, issued 2, November 2005, pages 131-140

Frieden, Jeffry, "*Global Capitalism: It's Fall and Rise in the Twentieth Century*", W.W. Norton and Company, New York 2006

ARTHUR JACKSON

G

H

Harlan, Jack R, and Zohary, Daniel, "*Distribution of Wild Wheats and Barley*", Science Vol. 153 September 1996

Harmon, Katherine. "*When Grasshoppers Go Biblical: Serotonin Causes Locusts to Swarm. A common brain chemical could be behind the process that morphs timid grasshoppers into voracious locusts.*" http://www.scientificamerican.com/article.cfm?id=when-grasshoppers-go-bibl

Harpending, Henry, and Alan R. Rogers. "*Genetic Perspectives on Human Origins and Differentiation.*" Annual Review of Genomics *and Human Genetics* 1 (2000): 361-385.

Food , Energy , and Water

Harpending, Henry C., et al. "The Genetic Structure of Ancient Human Populations." *Current Anthropology* 34 (1993): 483-496.

Hawks, John., Wang, Eric T., Cochran, Gregory M., Harpending, Henry C., Moyzis, Robert K., *Recent acceleration of human adaptive evolution* Department of Anthropology, University of Wisconsin–Madison, Madison, WI 53706,†Advanced Development, Affymetrix, Inc., Santa Clara, CA 95051,‡Department
of Anthropology, University of Utah, Salt Lake City, UT 84112, and ¶Department of Biological Chemistry and Institute of Genomics and Bioinformatics, University of
California, Irvine, Irvine CA 92697
Submitted to Proceedings of the National Academy of Sciences of the United States of America

Hewitt, Godfrey   *"The genetic legacy of the Quaternary ice ages"* Nature, Volume 405, June 200

Hewitt, G. M. *" Speciation and its Consequences"* (eds. Otte, D. & Endler, J.) 85–110 (Sinauer Associates, Sunderland, MA, 1989).

ARTHUR JACKSON

Hirst,   K.   Kris   ,   About.com   Guide,
http://archaeology.about.com/od/domestications/a/pla
nt_domestic.htm

I

Imperial College London (2007, March 25). *"New Evidence
Puts 'Snowball Earth'* Theory Out In The Cold" *ScienceDaily.*
Retrieved February 21,

J

Jorde, Lynn B., Michael Bamshad, and Alan R. Rogers. *"Using
Mitochondrial and Nuclear DNA Markers to Reconstruct Human
Evolution." BioEssays* 20 (1998): 126-136.

K

Ke, Yuehai, et al. *"African Origin of Modern Humans in East
Asia: A Tale of 12,000Y Chromosomes." Science*(2001): 1151-
1153.

Food , Energy , and Water

Krugman,   Paul.,   *Grains   Gone   Wild*
http://www.nytimes.com/2008/04/07/opinion/07krugman.html?_
r=1&hp=&pagewanted=print

L

Lahr, Marta. *The Evolution of Modern Human Diversity.* Cambridge, U.K.: Cambridge University Press, 1996.

Larson, Christina," *Why Some Cities Are Getting Drier as Skyscrapers Rise"* By Environment: Yale MagazinePosted on February 17, 2009, Printed on April 14, 2010 http://www.alternet.org/story/127457/

Lewin, Roger, Science, new series, volume 239, #484 March 5, 1911 1988, pages 1240-1241.

M

Malthus, Thomas; *An Essay on the Principle of Population*, 1798, an essay on the principle of population, as it affects the future improvement of society with remarks on the speculations of mr. godwin, m. ndorcet, and other writers.

Melville, Kate., *Modern man In Evolutionary fast lane*, http://www.scienceagogo.com/news/20071110211106data_trun c_sys.shtml

Mundell, Robert., " *Flexible Exchange Rates and Employment Policy*', The American Economic Review, 1961

Mundell, Robert., " *Capital Mobility and Stabilization Policy under Fixed and Flexible Exchange Rates*" The American Economic Review, 1963

Munro, Natalie D., *"Small Game, the Younger Dryas, and the Transition to Agriculture in the Southern Levant "* Mittelungen 12.indd 47, 2003

N

O

Ogle, B.M. and Grivetti, L.E. 1995. Legacy of the chamaleon: edible wild plants in the Kingdom of Swaziland, Southern Africa. A cultural , ecological, nutritional study. Part II- Demographics, species availability and dietary use, analyses by ecological zone. Ecology of Food and Nutrition 17:1-30.

P

Padulosi, S., Hodgkin, T., Williams J.T., and HaqInternational, N; *Estimates of number of plant species used around the world*, Plant Genetic Resources Institute (IPGRI), Rome, Italy; International Centre for Underutilized Crops (ICUC), Southampton, UK

Padulosi, S. 1999b. Criteria for priority setting in initiatives dealing with underutilized crops in Europe. Pp. 236-247 *in* Implementation of the Global Plan of Action in Europe – Conservation and Sustainable Utilization of Plant Genetic Resources for Food and Agriculture. (T. Gass, F. Frese, E. Begemann and E. Lipman, compilers), Proceedings of the European Symposium, 30 June-3 July 1998, Braunschweig, Germany. International Plant Genetic Resources Institute, Rome. 396 pp.

Padulosi, S. 1999c. Partners and partnership. *In* Enlarging the Basis of Food Security: the Role of Underutilized Species (Swaminathan M.S., ed.). International Workshop held at the M.S. Swaminathan Research Foundation, 17-19 February 1999, Chennai, India (in press).

ARTHUR JACKSON

Padulosi, S., P. Eyzaguirre and T. Hodgkin. 1999. Challenges and strategies in promoting conservation and use of underutilized and neglected species. Pp. 140-145 *in* Perspective on New Crops and New Uses (J. Janick, ed.), Proceedings of the Fourth National Symposium on New crops and New Uses. Biodiversity and Agricultural Sustainability, 8-11 November 1998, Phoenix, Arizona.

Paroda, R.S. and Bhag Mal.1993. Developing a National Programme for Research on Underutlized crops in India. Proceedings of the First International Crop Science Congress, Ames Iowa, USA 14-22 July 1992.

Pimpini, F. and M. Enzo. 1997. *Present and future prospects for rocket cultivation in the Veneto region.* Pp. 51-66 *in* Rocket: an old Mediterranean crop for the world (S. Padulosi and D. Pignone, eds.). Report of the II International Workshop on Rocket 13 December 1996, Padova, Italy. International Plant Genetic Resources Institute, Rome, Italy.

Pistorius, R. 1997. *Scientists, Plants and Politics – A history of the Plant Genetic Resources*
Movement. International Plant Genetic Resources Institute, Rome, Italy. 134 pp.
Paroda, R.S. and Bhag Mal. 1989. *New Plant Sources for Food and Industry in India.* Pp. 135-149 *in* New Crops for Food and Industry (G.E. Wickens, N. Haq and P. Day,

214

Food , Energy , and Water

eds.). Southampton, UK.

Q

R

Rafalski, Antoni, and Moerganti, Michele. *"Corn and humans: recombination and leakage of disequilibrium into genomes of similar size"* trends in Genetics, volume 20 no 2 February 2004

Remington, C. L. *"Suture-zones of hybrid interaction between recently joined biotas"* . *Evol. Biol.* **2,** 321–428 (1968).

Roberts, D. F.: *Body Weight, Race and Climate. Am J Phys Anthropol,* 1953. **11**: 533-558.

Rockström, J., W. Steffen, K. Noone, Å. Persson, F. S. Chapin, III, E. Lambin, T. M. Lenton, M. Scheffer, C. Folke, H. Schellnhuber, B. Nykvist, C. A. De Wit, T. Hughes, S. van der Leeuw, H. Rodhe, S. Sörlin, P. K. Snyder, R. Costanza, U. Svedin, M. Falkenmark, L. Karlberg, R. W. Corell, V. J. Fabry, J. Hansen, B. Walker, D. Liverman, K. Richardson, P. Crutzen, and J. Foley. 2009. " *Planetary boundaries:exploring the safe operating space for humanity. Ecology and Society* ", **14**(2): 32. [online]   URL: http://www.ecologyandsociety.org/vol14/iss2/art32/

Rosen, Arelene Miller, "*Civilizing Climate*", Rowman and Littlefield publishers, 2007

S

Spiegelman, Derek, " *most species are not driven to extinction before genetic factors impact them*", www.pnas.org , vol 101, Oct 2004

Strogatz, Steven. *Sync: The Emerging Science Of Spontanous Order,* Penguin Press 2003

Swanson, Peter. , "*Water: The Drop Of Life*", North Word Press, 2001.

T

Tainter, J. A. 1988. *The Collapse of Complex Societies.* Cambridge: Cambridge University Press.

Tainter, J. A. 1992. *Evolutionary consequences of war. In Effects of War on Society,* ed. G. Ausenda, pp. 103-130. San Marino: Center for Interdisciplinary Research on Social Stress.

Tainter, J. A. 1994a. *Southwestern contributions to the*

understanding of core-periphery relations. In Understanding Complexity in the Prehistoric Southwest, eds. G. J. Gumerman, and M. Gell-Mann, pp. 25-36. Santa Fe Institute, Studies in the Sciences of Complexity, Proceedings Volume XVI. Reading: Addison-Wesley.

U

Underhill, Peter A., et al. "Y Chromosome Sequence Variation and the History of Human Populations." Nature Genetics 26 (2000): 358-361.

V

Vane-Wright R.I, Humphries C.J, Williams P.H., What to protect? Systematics and the agony of choice. Biol. Conserv. 1991;55:235–254. doi:10.1016/0006-3207(91)90030-D

W

Williams, D., Dunkerley, D., DeDeckker, P., Kershaw, P. & Chappell, M. Quaternary Environments(Arnold, London, 1998).

ARTHUR JACKSON

Wilkinson, Richard "**The impact of inequality: How to make sick societies healthier**", Publisher, The New Press, 2006. ISBN, 1595586601

Willis, Katherine J., Gillson, Lindsey, Knapp, Sandra, *Biodiversity hotspots through time: an introduction*, The royal Society Biological Sciences, February 28, 2007, pages 167-174

X

Y

Young K.R, León B. *Tree-line changes along the Andes: implications of spatial patterns and dynamics*. Phil. Trans. R. Soc. B. 2007;**362**:263–272. doi:10.1098/rstb.2006.1986 [PubMed]

INDEX

Food , Energy , and Water

ARTHUR JACKSON

www.ingramcontent.com/pod-product-compliance
Lightning Source LLC
Chambersburg PA
CBHW030004190526
45157CB00014B/413